PRIMARY

comprehension

A

Fiction and nonfiction texts

Science Fiction

Poetry

Mystery

Myth/Legend

Fable

Play

Adventure

Fantasy

Fairytale

Horror/Supernatural

Humorous

Published by Prim-Ed Publishing
www.prim-ed.com

6253C

48/5

PRIMARY COMPREHENSION *(Book A)*

Published by Prim-Ed Publishing 2006
Reprinted under licence by Prim-Ed Publishing 2006
Copyright© R.I.C. Publications® 2005
ISBN 1 84654 008 9

PR–6253

Additional titles available in this series:
PRIMARY COMPREHENSION *(Book B)*
PRIMARY COMPREHENSION *(Book C)*
PRIMARY COMPREHENSION *(Book D)*
PRIMARY COMPREHENSION *(Book E)*
PRIMARY COMPREHENSION *(Book F)*
PRIMARY COMPREHENSION *(Book G)*

Internet websites
In some cases, websites or specific URLs may be recommended. While these are checked and rechecked at the time of publication, the publisher has no control over any subsequent changes which may be made to webpages. It is *strongly* recommended that the class teacher checks *all* URLs before allowing students to access them.

View all pages online

Website: www.prim-ed.com
Email: sales@prim-ed.com

PRIMARY COMPREHENSION

Foreword

Primary comprehension is a series of seven books designed to provide opportunities for pupils to read texts in a variety of fiction, poetry and nonfiction genres, to answer questions at literal, deductive and evaluative levels and to practise a variety of selected comprehension strategies.

Titles in this series include:

- *Primary Comprehension* Book A
- *Primary Comprehension* Book B
- *Primary Comprehension* Book C
- *Primary Comprehension* Book D
- *Primary Comprehension* Book E
- *Primary Comprehension* Book F
- *Primary Comprehension* Book G

Contents

Teachers Notes

Twenty different texts from a variety of genres are given. These include humour, fantasy, a myth/legend, folktale, mystery, adventure, horror/supernatural, fairytale, play, fable, science fiction, poetry and informational texts/nonfiction such as a timetable, letter, report, procedure, poster, map, programme, book cover and cartoon.

Three levels of questions are used to indicate the reader's comprehension of each text.

One or more particular comprehension strategies has been chosen for practice with each text.

Each text is given over four pages. Each group of four pages consists of:

~ a teachers page

~ pupil page – 1   (which always includes the text and sometimes literal questions)

~ pupil page – 2   (which gives literal, deductive and evaluative questions)

~ pupil page – 3   (which concentrates on the chosen comprehension strategy/ strategies)

Teachers page

The **title of the text** is given.

The particular **genre** is given.

Question types and comprehension strategies refer to the three levels of questioning and any particular strategies used.

Worksheet information details any background information required by the teacher about the genre or subject of the text or specific details regarding the use of the worksheets.

Answers are always given for literal questions and for deductive questions where appropriate. Answers for evaluative questions are best checked by the teacher following, or in conjunction with, class discussion.

Extension activities suggest titles of books or authors who write in the same genre, as well as other literacy activities relating to the text.

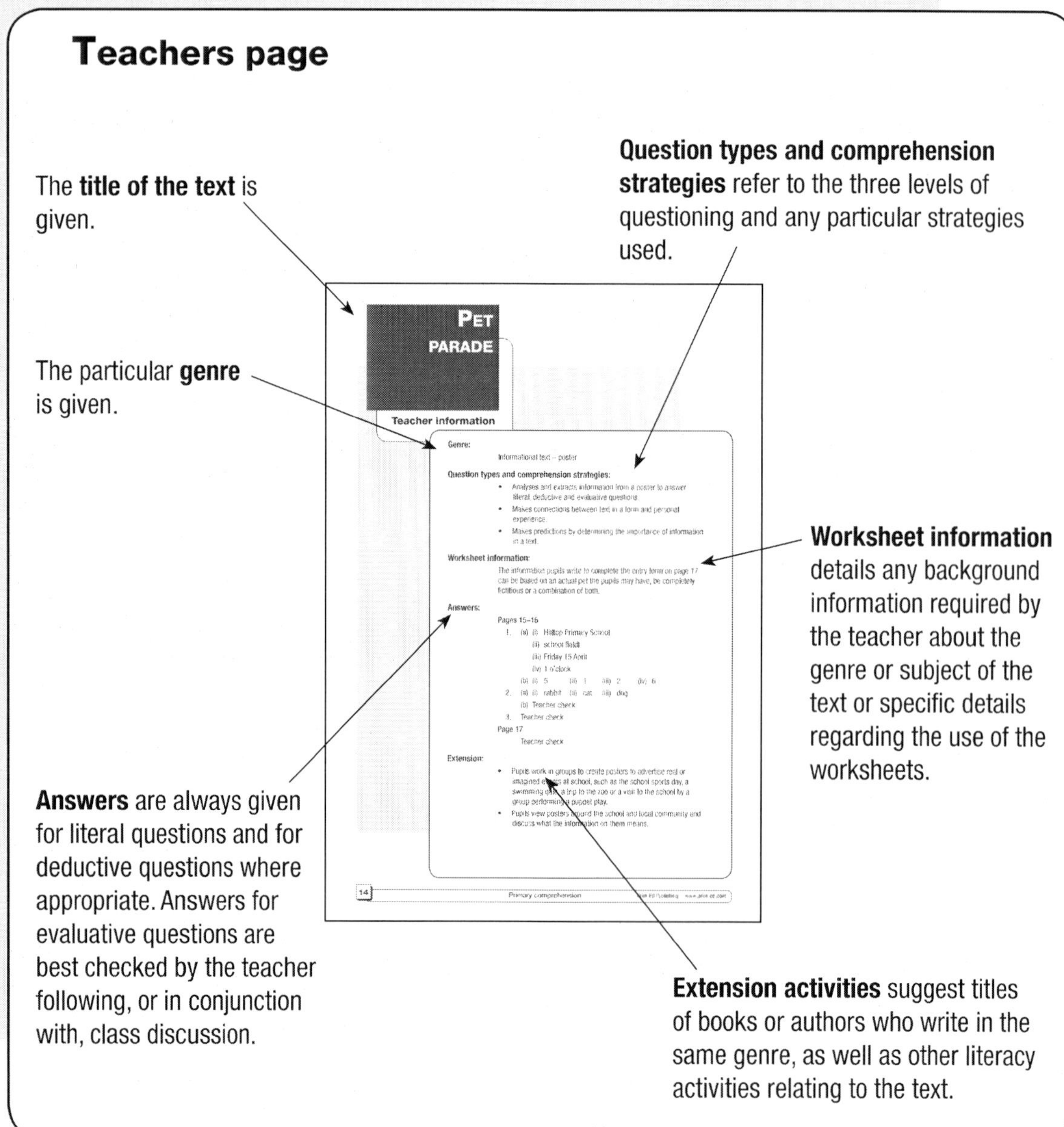

Primary comprehension

Prim-Ed Publishing   www.prim-ed.com

TEACHERS NOTES

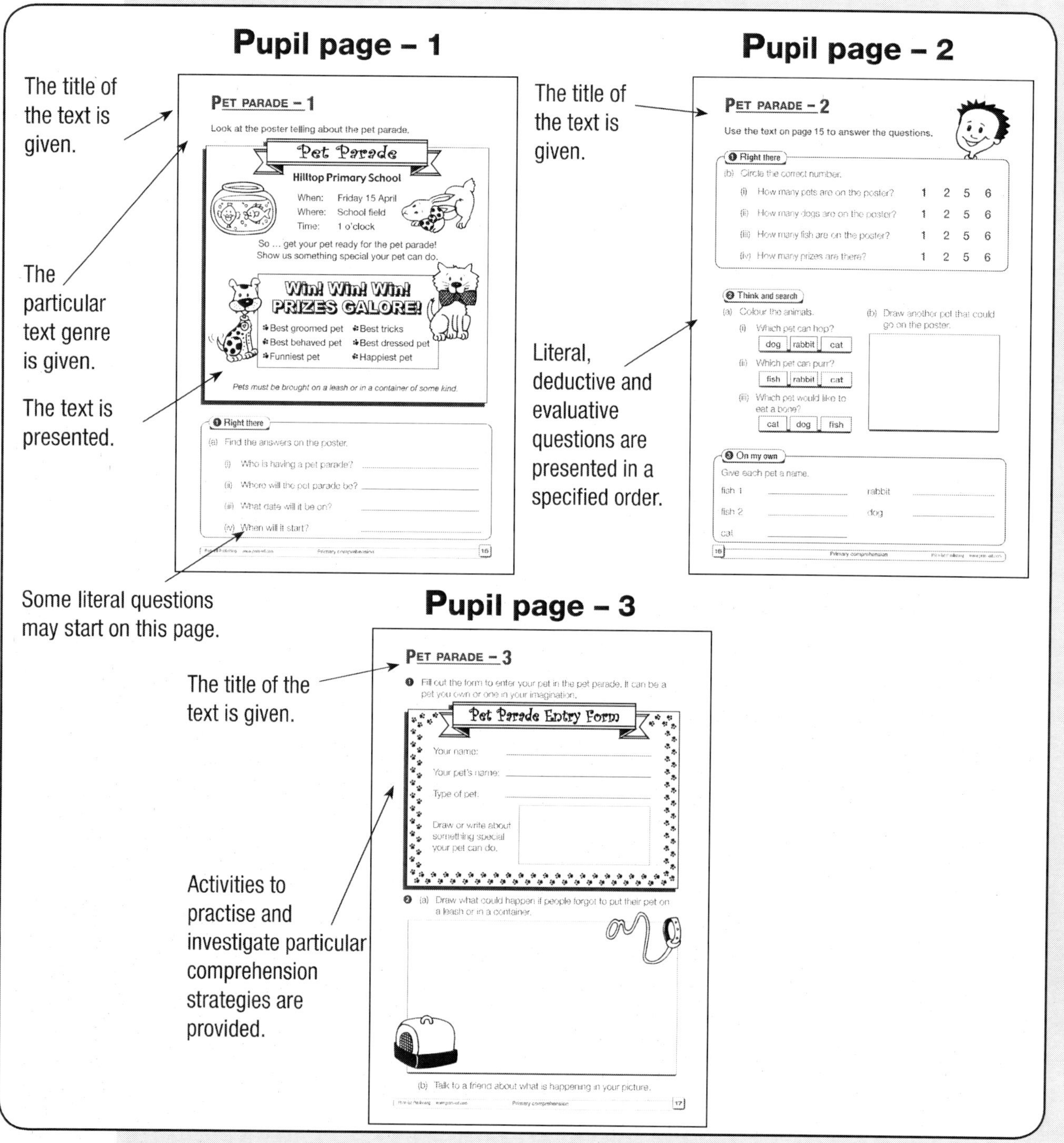

Types of questions

Pupils are given **three types (or levels) of questions** to assess their comprehension of a particular text in each genre:

- **Literal questions ('Right there')** are those which can be found directly in the text. These come first in the questions and are grouped.
- **Deductive (or inferential) questions ('Think and search')** follow the literal questions. Deductive questions are implied in the text and require the reader to read between the lines and think a bit more deeply about what has just been read.
- **Evaluative (or response/applied) questions ('On my own')** require the reader to think even further about the text and incorporate his/her personal experiences and knowledge to answer.

Answers for literal questions are always given and may be found on the teachers page. Answers for deductive questions are given where appropriate. Evaluative questions are best checked by the teacher following, or in conjunction with, class discussion.

TEACHERS **NOTES**

Comprehension strategies

Reading comprehension is an essential part of the reading process. Pupils need to comprehend what they read in order to become fluent readers.

The teacher is crucial in teaching and encouraging the use of comprehension strategies. Pupils' comprehension improves when teachers provide explicit instruction in comprehension strategies and when they implement activities that provide opportunities to practise and understand these strategies.

Several specific comprehension strategies have been selected for practice in this book.

Although specific examples have been selected, often other strategies, such as scanning, are used in conjunction with those indicated, even though they may not be stated. Rarely does a reader use a single strategy to comprehend a text.

Strategy definitions

Predicting

Prediction involves the pupils using illustrations, text or background knowledge to help them construct meaning. Pupils might predict what texts could be about, what could happen or how characters could act or react. Prediction may occur before, during and after reading, and can be adjusted during reading.

Pages 2–5, 6–9, and 14–17 use the strategy of predicting.

Making connections

Pupils comprehend texts by linking their prior knowledge and the new information given in the text. Pupils may make connections between the text and themselves, between the new text and other texts previously read, and between the text and the world.

Pages 10–13, 14–17, 18–21, 22–25, 26–29 and 30–33 use the strategy of making connections.

Comparing

This strategy is closely linked to the strategy of making connections. Pupils make comparisons by thinking more specifically about the similarities and differences between the connections being made.

Pages 34–37 and 38–41 use the strategy of comparing.

Sensory imaging

Sensory imaging involves pupils utilising all five senses to create mental images of passages in the text. Pupils use visual, auditory, olfactory, kinaesthetic or emotional images as well as their personal experiences to create these images. The images may help them to make predictions, form conclusions, interpret information and remember details.

Pages 22–25 and 42–45 use the strategy of sensory imaging.

Determining importance

The strategy of determining importance is particularly helpful when pupils are trying to comprehend informational texts. It involves pupils determining the important theme or main idea of particular paragraphs or passages.

As pupils become effective readers, they will constantly ask themselves what is most important in a phrase, sentence, paragraph, chapter or whole text. To determine importance, pupils will need to use a variety of information, such as the purpose for reading, their knowledge of the topic, background experiences and beliefs, and understanding of the text format.

Pages 46–49 and 50–53 use the strategy of determining importance.

TEACHERS **NOTES**

Strategy definitions

Skimming

Skimming is the strategy of looking quickly through texts to gain a general impression or overview of the content. Readers often use this strategy to quickly assess whether a text, or part of it, will meet their purpose. Because this book deals predominantly with comprehension after reading, skimming has not been included as one of the major strategies.

Scanning

Scanning is the strategy of quickly locating specific details such as dates, places or names, or those parts of the text which support a particular point of view. Scanning is often used but not specifically mentioned when used in conjunction with other strategies.

Pages 10–13, 26–29, 30–33, 54–57, 58–61, 66–69, 74–77 and 78–81 use the strategy of scanning.

Synthesising

Synthesising is the strategy which enables pupils to collate a range of information from a variety of sources in order to comprehend text. Pupils recall information, order details and piece information together to make sense of the text. Synthesising helps pupils to continually monitor their understanding of the text. Synthesising involves connecting, comparing, determining importance, posing questions and creating images.

Pages 58–61, 62–65 and 66–69 use the strategy of synthesising.

Paraphrasing/Summarising

Summarising involves the processes of recording key ideas, main points or the most important information from a text. Summarising or paraphrasing reduces a larger piece of text to the most important details.

Pages 50–53, 70–73, 74–77 and 78–81 use the strategy of summarising/paraphrasing.

Shared and guided reading

Shared and guided reading

Reading comprehension needs to be taught if pupils are to learn how to understand and engage with texts. The structure of comprehension lessons needs to provide direct teaching on the application of reading comprehension strategies.

Shared reading

To introduce the lesson, the teacher models reading the text, including a demonstration of how to use the comprehension strategies required by the specific unit of work. The demonstration might include:
- linking information in new text to prior knowledge
- generating mental images of parts of text
- asking 'why' questions
- pausing during reading and asking predictive questions

or any of the strategies outlined on pages vi and vii.

Guided reading

The pupils work in groups to complete the comprehension activities. The teacher works with and supports the pupils, prompting them to use different strategies to solve the questions; for example, the strategy modelled in the shared reading session should be applied to the text.

Plenary

Comprehension lessons should be concluded using a plenary session, giving the teacher and pupils the opportunity to discuss a range of issues, including:
- re-emphasis and practise of strategies
- clarification of misconceptions
- reflection and personal response
- explanation of how pupils solved particular questions
- presentation and discussion of work

Genre definitions

Fiction and poetry

Science fiction
These stories include backgrounds or plots based upon possible technology or inventions, experimental medicine, life in the future, environments drastically changed, alien races, space travel, gene engineering, dimensional portals or changed scientific principles. Science fiction encourages readers to suspend some of their disbelief and examine alternate possibilities.

Horror/Supernatural
Stories of this type are those which aim to make the reader feel fear, disgust or horror. A number of horror stories have become classics. These include *Frankenstein* by Mary Shelley, *Dracula* by Bram Stoker and *Dr Jekyll and Mr Hyde* by Robert Louis Stevenson.

Mystery stories
Stories of this kind focus on suspense and the solving of a mystery. Plots of mysteries often revolve around a crime, such as murder, theft or kidnapping. The hero must solve the mystery, overcoming unusual events, threats, assaults and often unknown forces or enemies. Stories about detectives, police, private investigators, amateur sleuths, spies, thrillers and courtroom dramas usually fall into this genre.

Fables
A fable is a short story which states a moral. Fables often use talking animals or animated objects as the main characters. The interaction of the animals or animated objects reveals general truths about human nature.

Fairytales
These tales are usually about elves, dragons, hobgoblins, sprites or magical beings and are often set in the distant past. Fairytales usually begin with the phrase 'Once upon a time ...' and end with the words ' ... and they lived happily ever after'. Charms, disguises and talking animals may also appear in fairytales.

Fantasy
A fantasy may be any text or story which is removed from reality. Stories may be set in nonexistent worlds such as an elf kingdom, on another planet or in alternate versions of the known world. The characters may not be human (dragons, trolls etc.) or may be humans who interact with non-human characters.

Folktales
Stories which have been passed from one generation to the next by word of mouth rather than being written down are folktales. Folktales may include sayings, superstitions, social rituals, legends or lore about the weather, animals or plants.

Plays
Plays are specific pieces of drama, usually enacted on a stage by a number of actors dressed in make-up and appropriate costumes.

Adventure stories
Exciting events and actions feature in these stories. Character development, themes or symbolism are not as important as the actions or events in an adventure story.

Humour
Humour involves characters or events which promote laughter, pleasure or humour in the reader.

Poetry
This is a genre which utilises rhythmic patterns of language. The patterns include meter (high and low stressed syllables), syllabification (the number of syllables in each line), rhyme, alliteration, or a combination of these. Poems often use figurative language.

Myths
These are stories which explain a belief, practice or natural phenomenon and usually involve gods, demons or supernatural beings. A myth does not necessarily have a basis in fact or a natural explanation.

Legends
Legends are told as though the events were actual historical events. Legends may or may not be based on an elaborated version of an historical event. Legends are usually about human beings, although gods may intervene in some way throughout the story.

Genre definitions

Nonfiction

Reports
Reports are written documents describing the findings of an individual or group. They may take the form of a newspaper report, sports or police report, or a report about an animal, person or object.

Letters
These are written conversations sent from one person to another. Letters usually begin with a greeting, contain the information to be related and conclude with a farewell signed by the sender.

Procedures
Procedures are instructions which tell how to make or do something. They use clear, concise language and command verbs. A list of materials required to complete the procedure is included and the instructions are set out in easy-to-follow steps.

Other **informational texts** such as **timetables**, **posters**, **programmes** and **maps** are excellent sources to teach and assess comprehension skills. Highly visual texts such as **book covers** and **cartoons** have been included because they provide the reader with other comprehension cues and are less reliant on word recognition.

CURRICULUM LINKS

England   Literacy Year 1

Texts / **Objectives**

Objectives	A scary story (2–5)	On the riverbank (6–9)	School assembly (10–13)	Pet parade (14–17)	Classroom (18–21)	The sad goblin (22–25)	The three little pigs (26–29)	Justin and the magic apples (30–33)	Thank you (34–37)	Russell the robot and his best buddy (38–41)	Action rhyme (42–45)	The wonderful birthday gift (46–49)	The sunflower (50–53)	The raven and the swan (54–57)	Why the bear has a stumpy tail (58–61)	Tilly Tidy-up (62–65)	How to make a pizza (66–69)	Cartoon (70–73)	The elephant (74–77)	A walk in the woods (78–81)
Term 1 — Read a range of fiction and poetry:																				
– stories with familiar settings																		●		●
– stories and rhymes with predictable and repetitive patterns	●	●																		
Read a range of nonfiction:																				
– labels					●															
– instructions																	●			
Text level work:																				
– read simple stories and poems independently	●	●																●		●
– describe story settings and incidents																				●
– recite stories and rhymes with predictable and repeating patterns	●	●																		
– re-enact stories in a variety of ways																				●
– read and use captions					●															
– read and follow simple instructions																	●			
– write and draw simple instructions																	●			
Term 2 — Read a range of fiction and poetry:																				
– traditional stories													●	●	●					
– fairy stories						●														
– action verses and rhymes											●									
– plays							●													
Read a range of nonfiction:																				
– non-chronological reports																			●	
Text level work:																				
– re-tell stories, giving the main points in sequence												●		●						
– identify and discuss characters						●								●						
– become aware of character and dialogue							●													
– recite simple poems and rhymes, with actions											●									
– predict what a book might be about from looking at front cover								●												
– use simple sentences to describe																			●	

Curriculum Links

England   Literacy Year 1

Objectives	A scary story (2–5)	On the riverbank (6–9)	School assembly (10–13)	Pet parade (14–17)	Classroom (18–21)	The sad goblin (22–25)	The three little pigs (26–29)	Justin and the magic apples (30–33)	Thank you (34–37)	Russell the robot and his best buddy (38–41)	Action rhyme (42–45)	The wonderful birthday gift (46–49)	The sunflower (50–53)	The raven and the swan (54–57)	Why the bear has a stumpy tail (58–61)	Tilly Tidy-up (62–65)	How to make a pizza (66–69)	Cartoon (70–73)	The elephant (74–77)	A walk in the woods (78–81)
Term 3 — • Read a range of fiction and poetry:																				
– stories about fantasy worlds										●		●								
– poems with patterned and predictable structures																●				
• Read a range of nonfiction:																				
– information texts				●																
– recounts of events			●						●											
• Text level work:																				
– read with sufficient concentration to complete a text				●						●		●								
– re-tell poems to give the main points in sequence																●				
– read recounts and begin to recognise generic structure			●	●					●											
– locate parts of text that give particular information			●	●					●											

Northern Ireland   English (Reading) Year 2

	A scary story (2–5)	On the riverbank (6–9)	School assembly (10–13)	Pet parade (14–17)	Classroom (18–21)	The sad goblin (22–25)	The three little pigs (26–29)	Justin and the magic apples (30–33)	Thank you (34–37)	Russell the robot and his best buddy (38–41)	Action rhyme (42–45)	The wonderful birthday gift (46–49)	The sunflower (50–53)	The raven and the swan (54–57)	Why the bear has a stumpy tail (58–61)	Tilly Tidy-up (62–65)	How to make a pizza (66–69)	Cartoon (70–73)	The elephant (74–77)	A walk in the woods (78–81)
Range — • engage with a range of texts, including:																				
– stories	●	●				●				●		●	●	●	●					●
– poems											●					●				
– plays								●												
– informational materials			●	●	●				●								●		●	
– environmental print				●	●				●											
– visual materials				●	●				●									●		
Purpose — • read for information	●	●	●	●	●	●	●	●	●	●	●	●	●	●	●	●	●	●	●	●
Reading activities — • take part in shared reading experiences	●	●	●	●	●	●	●	●	●	●	●	●	●	●	●	●	●	●	●	●
• retell/reread poems or stories		●												●		●	●			●
• make use of environmental print				●	●				●											
Expected outcomes — • begin to use evidence from the text to support their views	●	●	●	●	●	●	●	●	●	●	●	●	●	●	●	●	●	●	●	●
• show understanding of ways texts are structured by representing ideas through pictures and diagrams	●	●		●	●		●				●		●		●	●	●			●
• collect information relevant to specific purposes and represent their findings in a variety of ways	●	●		●	●	●	●		●	●	●	●	●	●	●	●	●	●	●	●

Curriculum Links

Republic of Ireland — English Language (Reading) — Senior Infant Class

Objectives		Pages 2–5 A scary story	Pages 6–9 On the riverbank	Pages 10–13 School assembly	Pages 14–17 Pet parade	Pages 18–21 Classroom	Pages 22–25 The sad goblin	Pages 26–29 The three little pigs	Pages 30–33 Justin and the magic apples	Pages 34–37 Thank you	Pages 38–41 Russell the robot and his best buddy	Pages 42–45 Action rhyme	Pages 46–49 The wonderful birthday gift	Pages 50–53 The sunflower	Pages 54–57 The raven and the swan	Pages 58–61 Why the bear has a stumpy tail	Pages 62–65 Tilly Tidy-up	Pages 66–69 How to make a pizza	Pages 70–73 Cartoon	Pages 74–77 The elephant	Pages 78–81 A walk in the woods
Receptiveness to language	• become familiar with a range of environmental print				●	●			●												
	• learn about basic terminology and conventions of books								●												
Competence and confidence	• experience the reading process being modelled	●	●	●	●	●	●	●	●	●	●	●	●	●	●	●	●	●	●	●	●
	• engage in shared reading activities	●	●	●	●	●	●	●	●	●	●	●	●	●	●	●	●	●	●	●	●
Developing cognitive abilities	• re-read and retell stories and poems		●				●							●		●	●				●
	• recall significant events and details in stories	●	●				●	●			●	●	●	●	●	●	●		●		●
	• analyse and interpret characters, situations, events and sequences presented pictorially	●	●	●	●		●	●		●			●	●	●	●	●	●	●	●	●
	• predict future incidents and outcomes in stories	●	●				●														
Emotional and imaginative development	• respond to characters, situations and story details, relating them to personal experience				●	●	●		●	●	●	●	●		●		●	●	●		●
	• record response to text through pictures and captions	●	●	●	●	●	●	●	●	●	●	●	●	●	●	●	●	●	●	●	●

Scotland — English Language (Reading) — Primary 2

Level A		Pages 2–5 A scary story	Pages 6–9 On the riverbank	Pages 10–13 School assembly	Pages 14–17 Pet parade	Pages 18–21 Classroom	Pages 22–25 The sad goblin	Pages 26–29 The three little pigs	Pages 30–33 Justin and the magic apples	Pages 34–37 Thank you	Pages 38–41 Russell the robot and his best buddy	Pages 42–45 Action rhyme	Pages 46–49 The wonderful birthday gift	Pages 50–53 The sunflower	Pages 54–57 The raven and the swan	Pages 58–61 Why the bear has a stumpy tail	Pages 62–65 Tilly Tidy-up	Pages 66–69 How to make a pizza	Pages 70–73 Cartoon	Pages 74–77 The elephant	Pages 78–81 A walk in the woods
	• Reading for information:																				
	– develop confidence in handling information	●	●	●	●	●	●	●	●	●	●	●	●	●	●	●	●	●	●	●	●
	– answer questions	●	●	●	●	●	●	●	●	●	●	●	●	●	●	●	●	●	●	●	●
	• Reading for enjoyment:																				
	– experience wide range of story and informational texts	●	●	●	●	●	●	●	●	●	●	●	●	●	●	●	●	●	●	●	●
	– teacher models good reading habits	●	●	●	●	●	●	●	●	●	●	●	●	●	●	●	●	●	●	●	●
	• Reading to reflect on the writer's ideas and craft:																				
	– discuss texts and answer questions	●	●	●	●	●	●	●	●	●	●	●	●	●	●	●	●	●	●	●	●
	– predict what might happen next	●	●		●		●														
	– pick out important ideas in a text	●	●	●	●	●	●	●	●	●	●	●	●	●	●	●	●	●	●	●	●
	• Awareness of genre:																				
	– look at covers, illustrations and titles								●												

CURRICULUM LINKS

Scotland — English Language (Reading) — Primary 2

Texts / **Objectives**

Level	Objective	A scary story (2–5)	On the riverbank (6–9)	School assembly (10–13)	Pet parade (14–17)	Classroom (18–21)	The sad goblin (22–25)	The three little pigs (26–29)	Justin and the magic apples (30–33)	Thank you (34–37)	Russell the robot and his best buddy (38–41)	Action rhyme (42–45)	The wonderful birthday gift (46–49)	The sunflower (50–53)	The raven and the swan (54–57)	Why the bear has a stumpy tail (58–61)	Tilly Tidy-up (62–65)	How to make a pizza (66–69)	Cartoon (70–73)	The elephant (74–77)	A walk in the woods (78–81)
Level B	**Reading for information:**																				
	– look at printed environmental text				●	●			●												
	– look at texts with practical purpose			●	●	●			●	●								●		●	
	– use wide selection of informational text			●	●	●												●			
	Reading for enjoyment:																				
	– experience fiction and poems with a variety of styles	●	●				●	●			●	●	●	●	●	●	●		●		●
	Reading to reflect on the writer's ideas and craft:																				
	– predict events	●	●		●			●													
	– answer questions	●	●	●	●	●	●	●	●	●	●	●	●	●	●	●	●	●	●	●	●
	– recall and refer to own experiences			●	●	●	●			●	●	●	●				●	●	●		●
	– sequence thoughts and ideas	●	●												●		●	●	●		●
	– respond through drawings and diagrams	●	●	●	●	●	●	●	●	●	●	●	●	●	●	●	●	●	●	●	●
	Awareness of genre:																				
	– predict the nature and content of a text								●												
	Knowledge about language:																				
	– be familiar with terms author and title								●												
	– discuss characters and scenes in fiction	●	●				●	●			●	●	●	●	●	●	●		●		●
	– encounter poems											●					●				

Wales — English (Reading) — Year 1

Range	Feature	A scary story (2–5)	On the riverbank (6–9)	School assembly (10–13)	Pet parade (14–17)	Classroom (18–21)	The sad goblin (22–25)	The three little pigs (26–29)	Justin and the magic apples (30–33)	Thank you (34–37)	Russell the robot and his best buddy (38–41)	Action rhyme (42–45)	The wonderful birthday gift (46–49)	The sunflower (50–53)	The raven and the swan (54–57)	Why the bear has a stumpy tail (58–61)	Tilly Tidy-up (62–65)	How to make a pizza (66–69)	Cartoon (70–73)	The elephant (74–77)	A walk in the woods (78–81)
Range	**Materials read should include these features:**																				
	– interesting subject matter and settings related to own experience or beyond everyday experience	●	●	●	●	●	●	●		●	●	●	●	●	●	●	●	●	●	●	●
	– language with recognisable repetitive patterns, rhyme and rhythm	●	●			●	●					●					●				
	– straightforward characterisation and plot	●	●				●	●			●		●	●	●	●					●
	– use of a variety of organisational and presentational techniques			●	●	●		●	●	●									●	●	
	Literature read should cover the following categories:																				
	– plays							●													
	– poems											●					●				

Primary comprehension

Curriculum links

Wales
English (Reading)
Year 1

Texts

Objectives

Category	Objective	A scary story Pages 2–5	On the riverbank Pages 6–9	School assembly Pages 10–13	Pet parade Pages 14–17	Classroom Pages 18–21	The sad goblin Pages 22–25	The three little pigs Pages 26–29	Justin and the magic apples Pages 30–33	Thank you Pages 34–37	Russell the robot and his best buddy Pages 38–41	Action rhyme Pages 42–45	The wonderful birthday gift Pages 46–49	The sunflower Pages 50–53	The raven and the swan Pages 54–57	Why the bear has a stumpy tail Pages 58–61	Tilly Tidy-up Pages 62–65	How to make a pizza Pages 66–69	Cartoon Pages 70–73	The elephant Pages 74–77	A walk in the woods Pages 78–81
Range	– stories with familiar settings																				●
	– stories based on imaginary or fantasy worlds										●		●								
	– traditional folk and fairy stories						●							●	●	●					
	– stories/poems containing patterned and predictable language	●	●				●	●				●					●				
	• Understand and respond to stories and poems, and in particular to:																				
	– talk about characters and events		●		●		●	●		●	●	●	●	●	●	●	●		●		●
	– say what might happen next in a story	●	●		●		●														
	– retell stories		●											●		●	●				●
Skills	• Use reference materials			●	●	●			●									●	●	●	

Teacher information

Genre:

Horror

Question types and comprehension strategies:

- Analyses and extracts information from a text to answer literal, deductive and evaluative questions.
- Predicts reasons for events happening.

Worksheet information:

- When reading the scary story with the pupils, teachers should accentuate the 'spooky' nature of the story by using a scary voice, putting emphasis on the words 'black' and speaking slowly until the last line, which may be spoken quickly, particularly when mentioning the mouse.

Answers:

Pages 3–4

1. (a) (i)   (in the) town
         (ii) black
         (iii) (on the) road
         (iv) (in the) truck
         (v)   a mouse

    (b) 'The mouse was in the box which was in the back of the truck sitting on the side of the road in the town.'

2. (a) It was a dark night.
    (b) The road was made from black tar.
    (c) He was looking for food.

3. mouse (1), box (2), truck (3), road (4), town (5)

Page 5

Teacher check

Extension:

- Other 'Not-so-scary' stories which may be read to pupils include:

    In a dark, dark wood by David A Carter
    Where the wild things are by Maurice Sendak
    There's a nightmare in my closet by Mercer Mayer
    A dark, dark tale by Ruth Brown

- Pupils may use the format of this short story to write one of their own.

A SCARY STORY – 1

Read the horror story.

In the black, black town

Was a black, black road.

On the black, black road

Was a black, black truck.

In the black, black truck

Was a black, black box.

In the black, black box

Was a … mouse!

---

❶ Right there

(a) Write words from the poem to answer the questions.

   (i)   Where was the road? ____________________________

   (ii)   What colour was the truck? ____________________

   (iii) Where was the truck? __________________________

   (iv) Where was the box? ___________________________

   (v)   What was in the box? _________________________

(b) Complete the long sentence by copying words from the story.

'The mouse was in the ______________________ which was in

the back of the ______________________ sitting on the side of the

______________________ in the ______________________.'

A <u>SCARY STORY – 2</u>

Use the text on page 3 to answer the questions.

② Think and search

Colour the words which best answer the question.

(a) Why was the town black?

| *The buildings were all painted black.* | *It was a dark night.* |

(b) Why was the road black?

| *The road was made from black tar.* | *The night was stormy.* |

(c) Why was the mouse hiding in the box?

| *He was looking for food.* | *He was travelling to another town.* |

③ On my own

Number the pictures from **1** to **5** (1 being the smallest thing and 5 the biggest thing).

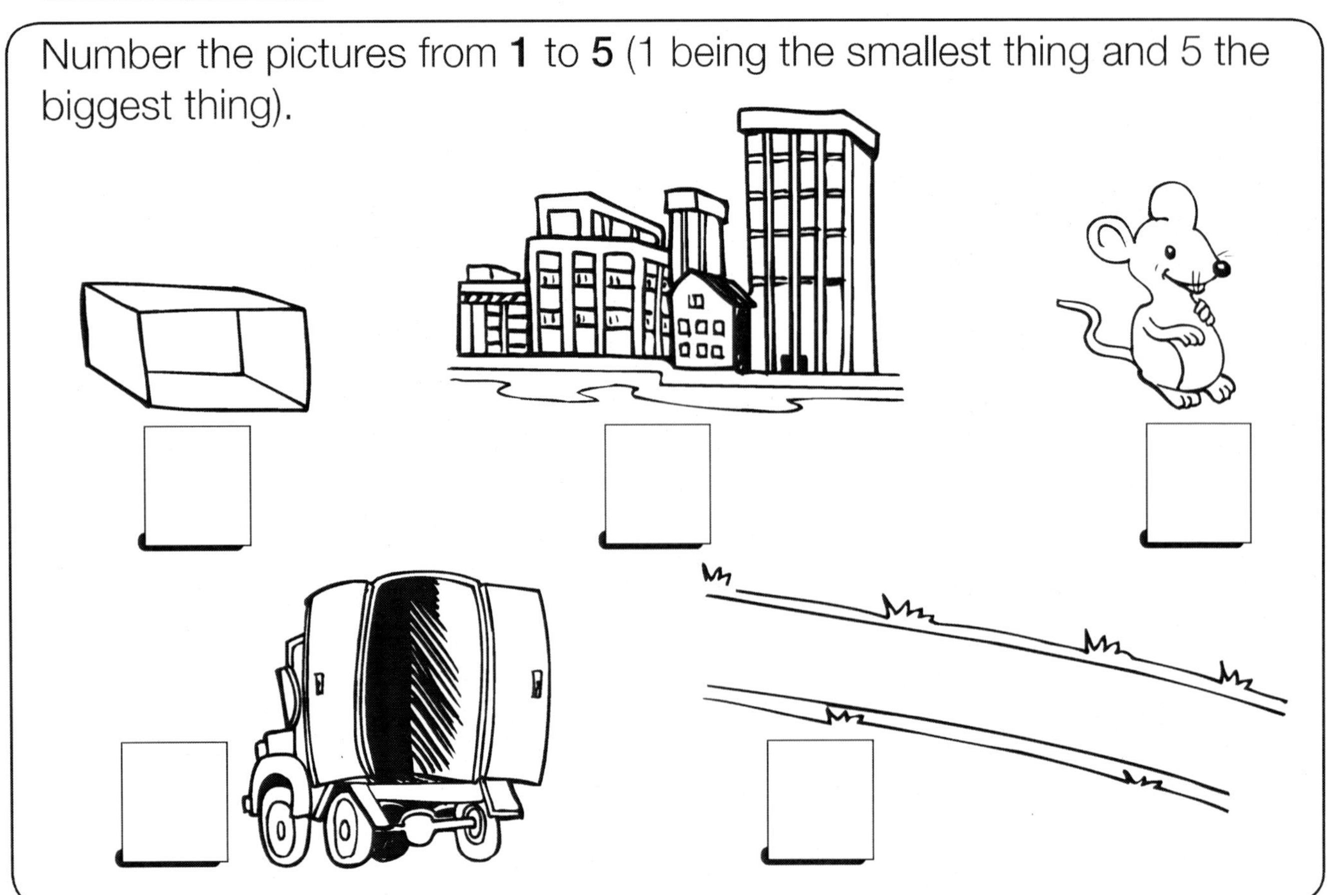

A <u>SCARY STORY – 3</u>

After reading the text on page 3, draw pictures or write words to predict what may have happened or will happen.

(a) Why was the truck in the town?

(b) Why was the truck on the road at night?

(c) Why did the truck stop?

(d) How did the mouse get into the box?

(e) How will the mouse stay alive in the box?

(f) How will the mouse get out of the truck?

On the Riverbank

Teacher information

Genre:

Mystery

Question types and comprehension strategies:

- Analyses and extracts information from a mystery text to answer literal, deductive and evaluative questions.
- Predicts future actions based on prior knowledge and reading of the text.

Worksheet information:

- Teachers may need to read instructions to the pupils, who can point to the words and follow the text.
- Some activities on page 8 require pupils to provide an explanation of their answers.

Answers:

Pages 7–8

1. (a) (i) no (ii) yes (iii) yes
   (b) 4 animals
2. Teacher check
3. Teacher check

Page 9

Teacher check

Extension:

- Pupils add their own actions and perform the story as a play.
- Create a mural of the animals in the story and other jungle animals.
- Use the story as the basis for text innovation; for example, 'Who left the clothes on the bathroom floor?'

ON THE RIVERBANK – 1

Read the mystery.

Who left the boat on the riverbank?

Lion, did you leave the boat on the riverbank?

No, I did not leave the boat on the riverbank, but I'll get in.

Monkey, did you leave the boat on the riverbank?

No, I did not leave the boat on the riverbank, but I'll hop in.

Tiger, did you leave the boat on the riverbank?

No, I did not leave the boat on the riverbank, but I'll jump in.

Elephant, did you leave the boat on the riverbank?

No, I did not leave the boat on the riverbank, but I'll climb in.

Crocodile, did you leave the boat on the riverbank?

Yes, I left the boat on the riverbank to catch my dinner.

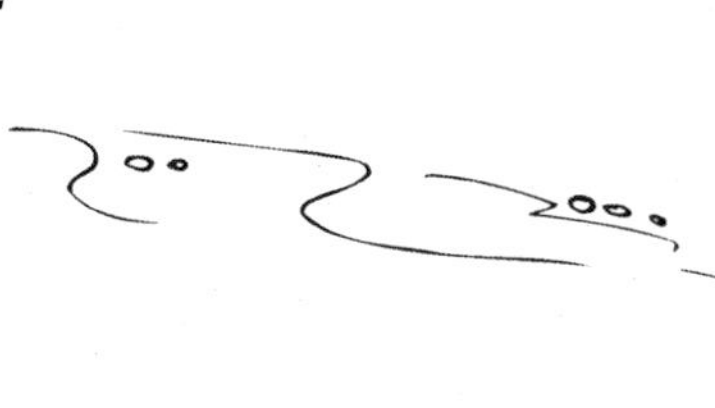

❶ Right there

(a) Colour **yes** or **no**.

   (i)   Crocodile got into the boat.   YES | NO

   (ii) Tiger got into the boat.   YES | NO

   (iii) Crocodile left the boat on the riverbank.   YES | NO

(b) How many animals got into the boat?

ON THE RIVERBANK – 2

Use the text on page 7 to answer the questions.

(a) Draw the cleverest animal in the story.

(b) What did he do?

(a) Draw the four animals in order from the heaviest to the lightest.

Heaviest

Lightest

(b) Will the boat sink? YES NO Why?

ON THE RIVERBANK – 3

1 Read then draw what happened.

(a) The boat is on the riverbank.

(b) Lion gets in.

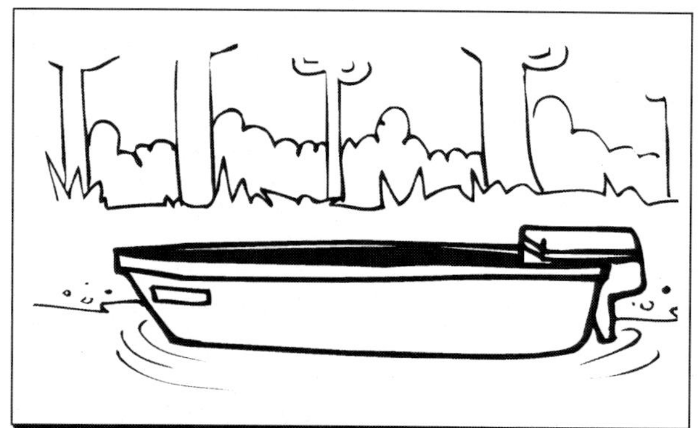

(c) Monkey hops in.

(d) Tiger jumps in.

(e) Elephant climbs in.

(f) The boat sinks.

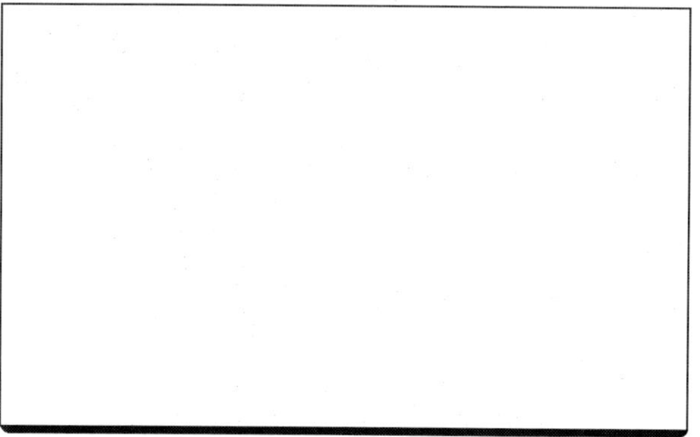

2 Draw what happens next.

Genre:

Informational text – programme

Question types and comprehension strategies:

- Analyses and extracts information from a programme to answer literal, deductive and evaluative questions.
- Makes connections between new text and his/her own experiences.
- Scans text to locate words.

Worksheet information:

- In order to complete page 12, pupils will need to know their own school headteacher and to understand something about his or her role in the school. They would benefit from the opportunity to ask questions, perhaps during a visit from the headteacher to their classroom for this specific purpose.
- Pupils need to be familiar with the fairytale genre and the story *The three billygoats Gruff*.
- Page 13 requires the pupils to illustrate a class performing a play. They will need to be familiar with this genre and to have some understanding of costuming etc.

Answers:

Pages 11–12

1. (a) no   (b) yes   (c) yes   (d) no   (e) yes
2. (a) true   (b) false   (c) true
3. (a) Teacher check
   (b) Teacher check

Page 13

Teacher check

Extension:

- Brainstorm information to produce a programme for a school assembly the class has recently attended with details about the order of events and who did what. Compare this assembly with the one at Sunnywell Primary School by listing similarities and differences.
- Read a number of different fairytales and discuss the parts played by the different characters, how they would speak and move, the costumes they might wear and the role of the storyteller.

Read the programme.

Sunnywell Primary School
Assembly programme
Friday 5 October

Introduced by:	Class 1
Welcome:	Luke
Hymn:	Mr Wilson (piano)
Announcements:	Mrs Andrews (deputy)
House points:	House captains
Awards:	Mr Green (headteacher)
Class item:	The three billy goats Gruff
	Class 1
Thank you:	Ben

❶ Right there

Colour **yes** or **no**.

(a) Mrs Andrews is the headteacher. YES | NO

(b) Class 1 are introducing the assembly. YES | NO

(c) Ben is going to say thank you at the end. YES | NO

(d) Mr Green will make the announcements. YES | NO

(e) Mr Wilson plays the piano. YES | NO

SCHOOL ASSEMBLY **– 2**

2 Think and search

Colour **true** or **false**.

(a) Luke and Ben are Class 1 pupils.

(b) The house captains are Class 1 pupils.

(c) Class 1 performed a play.

3 On my own

(a) (i) Draw a picture of your headteacher.

(ii) My headteacher's name is

_______________________________.

(iii) Where is your headteacher in your drawing?

____

(iv) What did you draw your headteacher doing?

____

____

(b) Complete these sentences about your headteacher.

(i) My headteacher is _______________________________.

(ii) I think my headteacher _______________________________.

Primary comprehension   Prim-Ed Publishing   www.prim-ed.com

Sᴄʜᴏᴏʟ Assembly – 3

1 The Class 1 item was the play about the three billy goats Gruff. Draw a picture of the children doing this play.

2 (a) What play would you like to do? ________________

(b) What part would you like to play? ________________

(c) Draw you and some of your class doing this play.

Teacher information

Genre:

Informational text – poster

Question types and comprehension strategies:

- Analyses and extracts information from a poster to answer literal, deductive and evaluative questions.
- Makes connections between text in a form and personal experience.
- Makes predictions by determining the importance of information in a text.

Worksheet information:

The information pupils write to complete the entry form on page 17 can be based on an actual pet the pupils may have, be completely fictitious or a combination of both.

Answers:

Pages 15–16

1. (a) (i)   Hilltop Primary School
       (ii) school field
       (iii) Friday 15 April
       (iv) 1 o'clock
   (b) (i) 5   (ii) 1   (iii) 2   (iv) 6
2. (a) (i) rabbit   (ii) cat   (iii) dog
   (b) Teacher check
3. Teacher check

Page 17

Teacher check

Extension:

- Pupils work in groups to create posters to advertise real or imagined events at school, such as the school sports day, a swimming gala, a trip to the zoo or a visit to the school by a group performing a puppet play.
- Pupils view posters around the school and local community and discuss what the information on them means.

PET PARADE – 1

Look at the poster telling about the pet parade.

Pet Parade

Hilltop Primary School

When: Friday 15 April

Where: School field

Time: 1 o'clock

So … get your pet ready for the pet parade!
Show us something special your pet can do.

Pets must be brought on a leash or in a container of some kind.

❶ Right there

(a)   Find the answers on the poster.

    (i)   Who is having a pet parade?   ______________________________

    (ii)   Where will the pet parade be?   ______________________________

    (iii) What date will it be on?   ______________________________

    (iv)   When will it start?   ______________________________

Pet parade – 2

Use the text on page 15 to answer the questions.

❶ Right there

(b) Circle the correct number.

    (i)   How many pets are on the poster?   **1   2   5   6**

    (ii)   How many dogs are on the poster?   **1   2   5   6**

    (iii) How many fish are on the poster?   **1   2   5   6**

    (iv) How many prizes are there?   **1   2   5   6**

❷ Think and search

(a) Colour the animals.

    (i)   Which pet can hop?

dog	rabbit	cat

    (ii) Which pet can purr?

fish	rabbit	cat

    (iii) Which pet would like to eat a bone?

cat	dog	fish

(b) Draw another pet that could go on the poster.

❸ On my own

Give each pet a name.

fish 1   ______________________   rabbit   ______________________

fish 2   ______________________   dog   ______________________

cat   ______________________

PET PARADE – 3

1   Fill out the form to enter your pet in the pet parade. It can be a pet you own or one in your imagination.

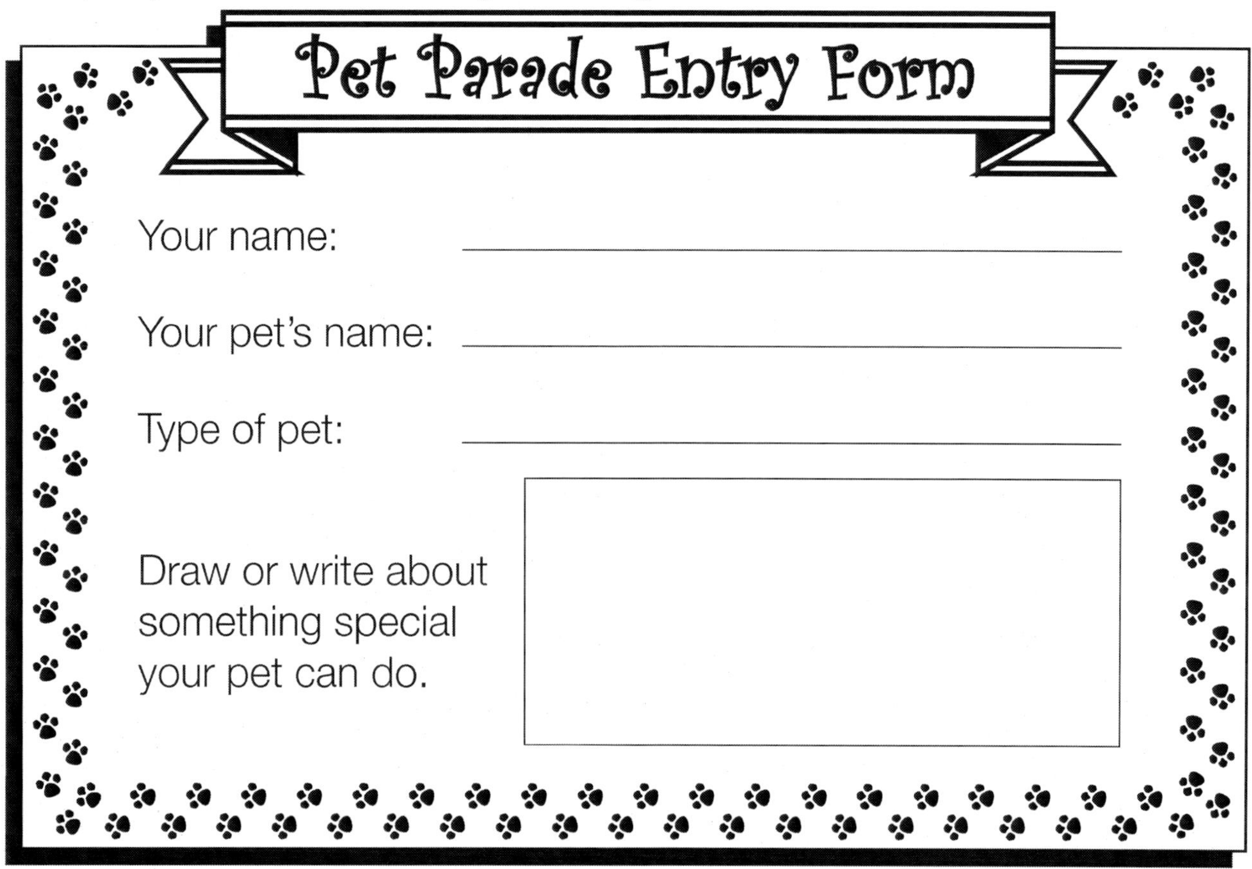

2   (a)   Draw what could happen if people forgot to put their pet on a leash or in a container.

      (b)   Talk to a friend about what is happening in your picture.

Teacher information

Genre:

Informational text – map

Question types and comprehension strategies:

- Analyses and extracts information from a map to answer literal, deductive and evaluative questions.
- Makes connections between a visual text and personal experience.

Worksheet information:

Before making a map of a classroom for the activity on page 21, pupils should cut out the items at the bottom of the page and then experiment by moving the pieces on the map before gluing them into position. They can then draw any other items they wish to include, such as extra desks, display boards and the positions of windows and doors.

Answers:

Pages 19–20

1. (a) (i) window   (ii) sink/hooks (iii) heater
        (iv) mat/board/cupboard/windows
    (b) (i) 1   (ii) 20   (iii) 2
    (c) (i) yes   (ii) no   (iii) yes
2. Teacher check
3. Teacher check

Page 21

Teacher check

Extension:

- Pupils work in pairs, and, using the maps they created, ask oral questions of each other, such as the relative positions of objects on their maps.
- Pupils view maps created by the teacher or make their own of the school, school playground, a bedroom or a park.

CLASSROOM **– 1**

Look at the map and read the labels.

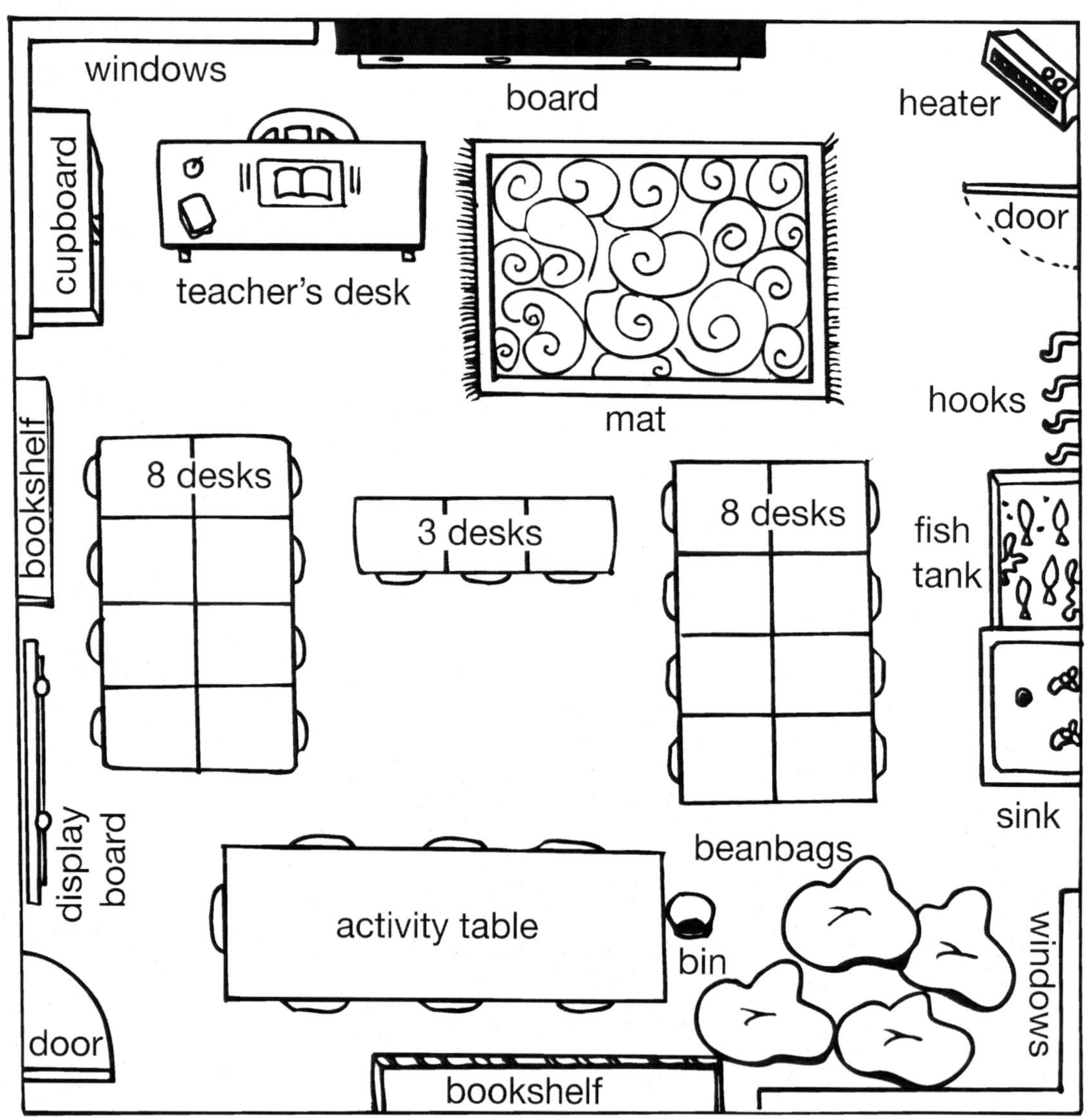

❶ Right there

(a)   Choose a label from the map.

   (i)   A cupboard is in front of the _________________________.

   (ii)   The fish tank is next to the _________________________.

   (iii)   The _________________________ is behind a door.

   (iv)   The teacher's desk is near the _________________________.

CLASSROOM – 2

Use the map on page 19 to answer the questions.

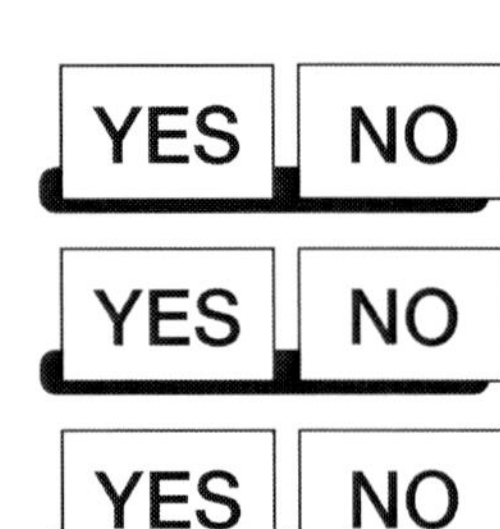

❶ Right there

(b) Circle the correct number.

   (i)   How many bins in the classroom?   1   2   20

   (ii) How many desks in the classroom?   1   2   20

   (iii) How many doors in the classroom?   1   2   20

(c) Colour **yes** or **no**.

   (i)   Is the display board near the activity table?   YES | NO

   (ii) Is the mat in front of the bookshelf?   YES | NO

   (iii) Are the windows in the corners?   YES | NO

❷ Think and search

(a) Where would be a good place to read a book?

____

(b) Where could you wash your hands?

____

❸ On my own

Draw two things you will not find in a classroom.

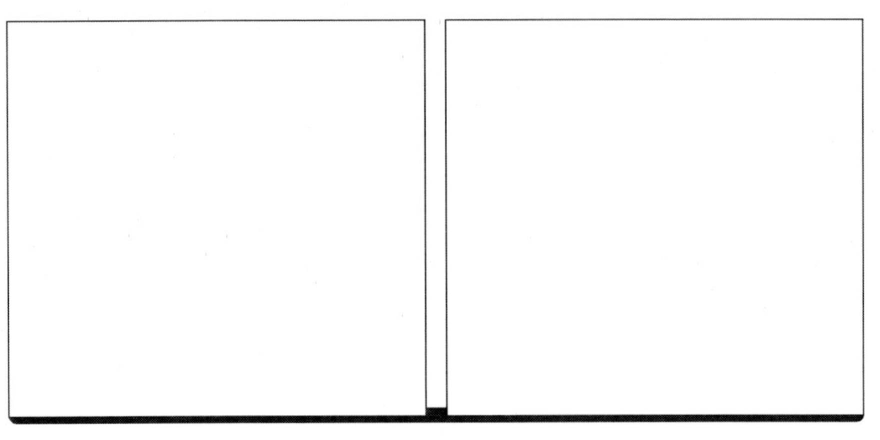

Classroom – 3

Make a map of a classroom using the pictures below.
Draw any other items you would like on your map.

sink

pupils' desks

fish tank

teacher's desk

beanbags

mat

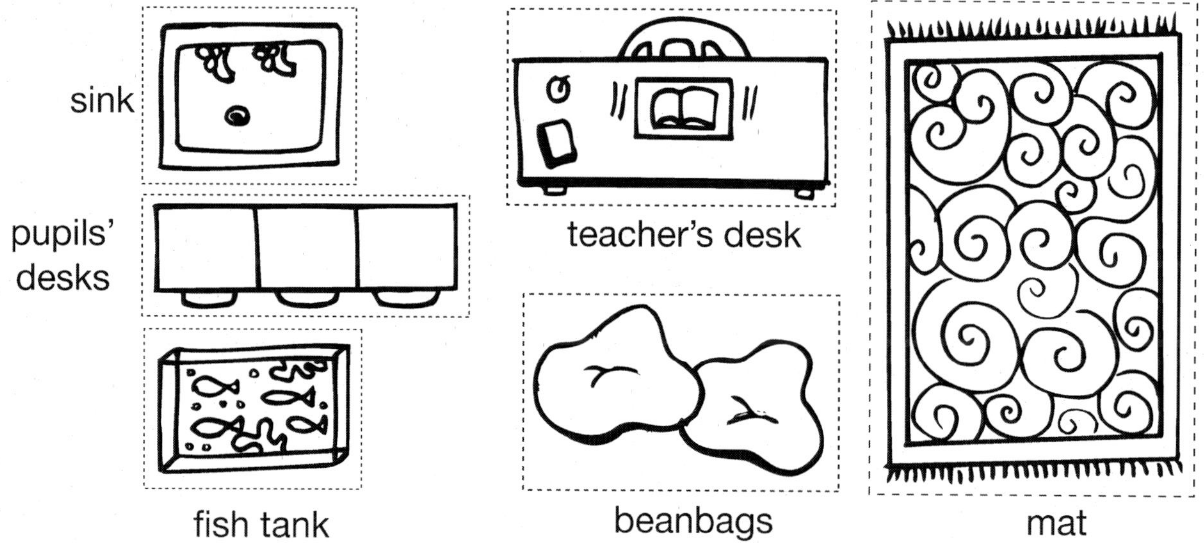

THE SAD GOBLIN

Teacher information

Genre:

Fairytale

Question types and comprehension strategies:

- Analyses and extracts information from a fairytale to answer literal, deductive and evaluative questions.
- Makes connections between new text and other known texts and his/her own experiences.
- Creates and recreates sensory images.

Worksheet information:

Pupils need to be familiar with the fairytale genre and the stories *The three little pigs*, *Snow White*, *Goldilocks* and *Little Red Riding Hood*.

Answers:

Page 24

1. (a) (i) smile (ii) looked (iii) fell
   (b) Snow White — seven dwarfs
       Goldilocks — three bears
       Little Red Riding Hood — the woods
2. Teacher check
3. Teacher check

Page 25

Teacher check

Extension:

- Brainstorm ideas and create a poster or collage about 'things that make people smile'.
- Read a variety of different fairytales and discuss different features; for example, how they start and finish, the good and bad characters and the things they do.
- Play 'Who am I?' giving the pupil clues about a well-known fairytale character to identify.

Read the fairytale.

The sad goblin

Once upon a time there was a very sad goblin called Sam, who lost his smile. He looked and looked but he could not find it.

He saw seven dwarfs and Snow White and asked,

'Have you seen my smile?'

'No, but we'll help you look for it', they said.

He saw three little pigs building houses and asked,

'Have you seen my smile?'

'No, but we'll help you look for it', they said.

He saw Little Red Riding Hood in the woods and asked,

'Have you seen my smile?'

'No, but I'll help you look for it', she said.

He saw Goldilocks and the three bears in their house and asked,

'Have you seen my smile?'

'No, but we'll help you look for it', they said.

They all looked here, they all looked there and they even looked deep down in the lake. Then they all fell in with a great big splash!

They looked so funny standing in the water dripping wet that Sam laughed and laughed. He laughed so much that he found his smile and they all lived happily ever after.

THE SAD GOBLIN – 2

Use the text on page 23 to answer the questions.

❶ Right there

(a) Find the missing word. | *fell* | *smile* | *looked* |

   (i)   Sam lost his ___________.

   (ii) The three pigs ___________ for Sam's smile.

   (iii) They all ___________ in the lake.

(b) Draw lines to match these.

Snow White		three bears
Goldilocks		seven dwarfs
Little Red Riding Hood		the woods

❷ Think and search

Colour **yes** or **no**.

(a) Sam had lots of friends.   YES / NO

(b) Sam's friends wanted to help him.   YES / NO

(c) Sam's smile was in the lake.   YES / NO

(d) Sam wanted to be sad.   YES / NO

(e) Do you think Sam will keep his smile?   YES / NO

❸ On my own

Draw and write about someone who helps you.

My helper's name is ___________

My helper ___________

____

THE SAD GOBLIN – 3

Use the text on page 23 to complete the activity.

❶ Draw or write about Sam to complete the boxes below.

(a) What/Who did Sam see?

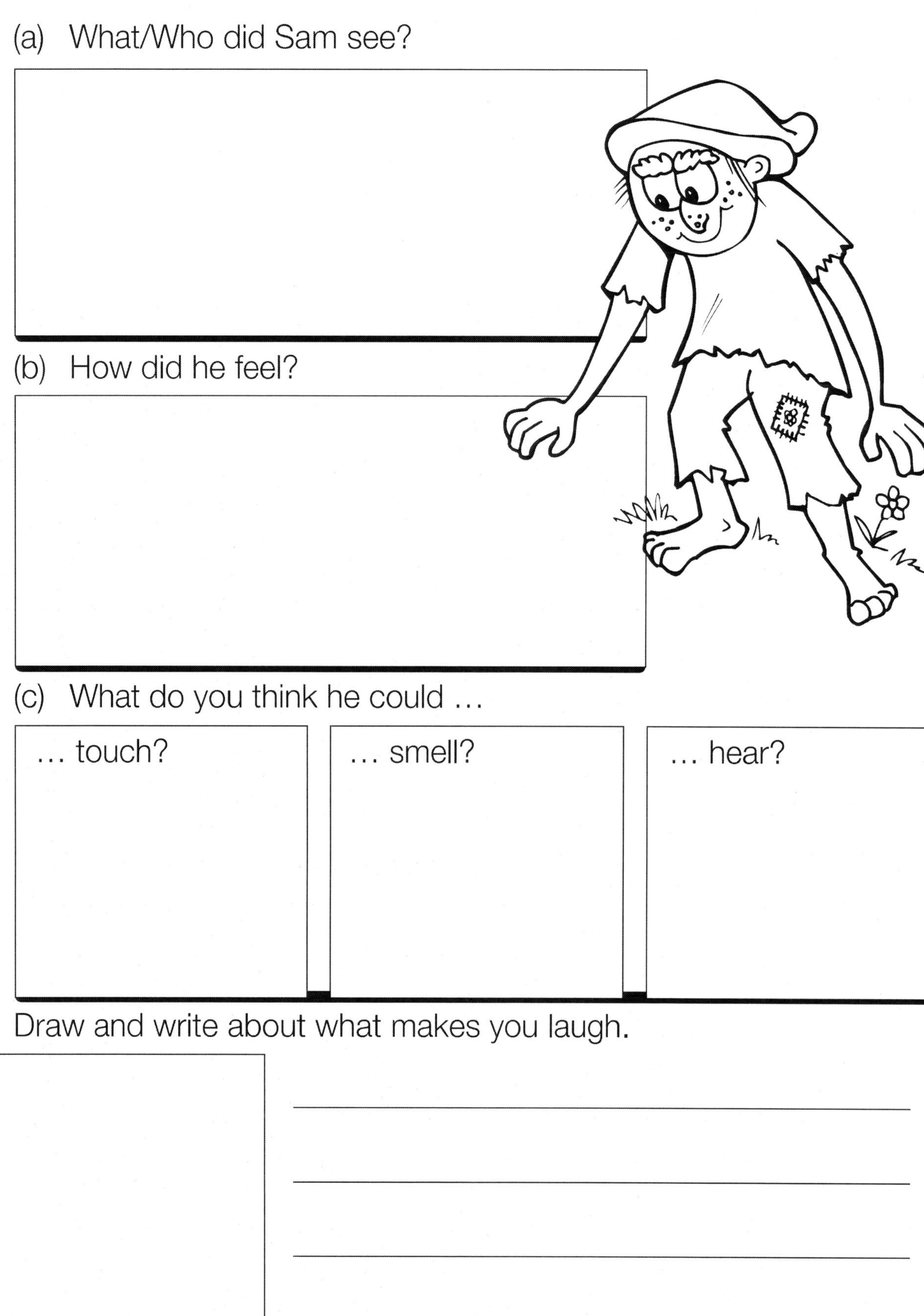

(b) How did he feel?

(c) What do you think he could …

… touch?

… smell?

… hear?

❷ Draw and write about what makes you laugh.

Teacher information

Genre:

Play

Question types and comprehension strategies:

- Analyses and extracts information from a play to answer literal, deductive and evaluative questions.
- Scans for relevant information.
- Makes connections based on prior knowledge and the text to predict feelings and reactions of characters.

Worksheet information:

- The familiar story *The three little pigs*, with its easily remembered repetition, has been chosen to enable all early readers to 'read' the parts with relative ease. A more able reader is needed for the part of the storyteller.
- Teachers should read all instructions to the pupils as they point to the words or follow the line of words being read.
- Pupils would benefit from opportunities to show the houses they design and draw to others and to explain particular features and the reasons for their inclusion.

Answers:

Page 28

1. (a) yes   (b) no   (c) no   (d) yes   (e) yes
2. Teacher check
3. Teacher check

Page 29

Teacher check

Extension:

- Pupils construct houses using a variety of different materials.
- Readers theatre—using familiar text and different coloured highlighter pens for each part.
- Collect, display and read a variety of different *Three little pigs* books.

THE THREE LITTLE PIGS – 1

Read the play.

Storyteller:	*Once upon a time there was a big bad wolf who was very hungry. He went to the house made of straw and said to the first little pig:*
Wolf:	*Little pig, little pig, let me in.*
First Little Pig:	*No, by the hair of my chinny-chin-chin, I will not let you in.*
Wolf:	*Then I'll huff and I'll puff and I'll blow your house in.*
Storyteller:	*So he huffed and he puffed and he blew the house in. The first little pig ran to the second little pig's house made of sticks. The wolf followed him.*
Wolf:	*Little pig, little pig, let me in.*
Second Little Pig:	*No, by the hair of my chinny-chin-chin, I will not let you in.*
Wolf:	*Then, I'll huff and I'll puff and I'll blow your house in.*
Storyteller:	*So he huffed and he puffed and he blew the house in. The two little pigs ran to the third little pig's house made of bricks. The wolf followed them.*
Wolf:	*Little pig, little pig, let me in.*
Third Little Pig:	*No, by the hair of my chinny-chin-chin, I will not let you in.*
Wolf:	*Then I'll huff and I'll puff and I'll blow your house in.*
Storyteller:	*So he huffed and he puffed and he huffed and he puffed, but he could not blow the house in.*
Third Little Pig:	*Let's get a big pot of hot water.*
Storyteller:	*The wolf climbed onto the roof and came down the chimney. He fell into the pot of water and that was the end of the big bad wolf.*

THE THREE LITTLE PIGS – 2

Use the text on page 27 to answer the questions.

❶ Right there

Colour **yes** or **no**.

(a) The wolf was hungry. YES / NO

(b) The wolf ate the pigs. YES / NO

(c) The pigs let the wolf in. YES / NO

(d) The wolf fell in the pot. YES / NO

(e) The wolf blew down the straw house. YES / NO

❷ Think and search

How do you think the pigs were feeling?

Put a tick or a cross next to each word.

frightened ☐   happy ☐

scared ☐   worried ☐

sad ☐   glad ☐

surprised ☐   angry ☐

❸ On my own

Draw the wolf in the hot pot.

THE THREE LITTLE PIGS – 3

1 Two little pigs do not have a house to live in. Draw a house that you think one of the pigs would like to build, then tell about the house.

(a) The house is made of ________________________________.

(b) The ________________________ little pig will live in it.

(c) The house has ______________ doors.

(d) It has ______________ windows.

(e) I like the house because ________________________

____

JUSTIN AND THE MAGIC APPLES

Teacher information

Genre:

Informational visual text — book cover

Question types and comprehension strategies:

- Analyses and extracts information from a visual text (a book cover) to answer literal, deductive and evaluative questions.
- Scans for relevant information.
- Makes connections between a book cover viewed and one to be created.
- Makes connections between a book cover and self.

Worksheet information:

- Pupils need to be able to comprehend visual texts at this stage of their reading life as they are still learning the strategies needed to comprehend written texts. A book cover has been chosen as the example for this visual text.
- The activities chosen require very little reading ability; however, adult assistance may be needed at times for the odd unfamiliar word.
- Teachers should read all instructions to the pupils while the pupils point to the words or follow the line of words being read.
- Pupils will need some understanding of what an author is and what an illustrator does in order to answer Question 2 on page 32.

Answers:

Pages 31–32

1. (a) (i) Ian Celson   (ii) Amy White   (iii) Justin and the magic apples
   (b) (i) Justin   (ii) apples   (iii) happy
2. (a) Ian Celson — author   Amy White — illustrator
   (b) Teacher check
3. Teacher check

Page 33

Teacher check

Extension:

- Pupils view a variety of different types of book covers including nonfiction and fiction books, comic books, newspapers and magazines for comparison.
- Pupils use art lessons to create patterned covers for class books or folders.
- Display covers of books which adults read and discuss the differences between those and books written especially for young children.

JUSTIN AND THE MAGIC APPLES – 1

Read the book cover below.

❶ Right there

(a) Copy words from the book cover to answer the questions.

(i) Who wrote the book? _______________________

(ii) Who drew the pictures for the book?

____

(iii) What is the title of the book?

____

Justin and the Magic Apples – 2

Use the text on page 31 to answer the questions.

❶ Right there

(b) Colour the correct word.

(i) The name of the boy in the book is | Justin | Ian |.

(ii) The magic fruit in the book is | bananas | apples |.

(iii) Justin is | happy | sad | to receive the magic apples.

❷ Think and search

(a) Draw lines to match the name to the person's correct title.

Ian Celson•   •illustrator

Amy White•   •author

(b) Colour **yes** or **no** to answer the questions.

(i) Amy White is a good drawer.   YES / NO

(ii) The story is going to be interesting.   YES / NO

(iii) Justin has done something good to get the magic apples.   YES / NO

❸ On my own

Draw a picture to show what the magic apples will do for Justin.

1 Use the book cover on page 31 to help you make up a book cover of your own. Tick the boxes when you have put in all the different parts.

book title ☐

cover illustration ☐

name of author ☐

name of illustrator ☐

2 Write words to tell what you would like magic apples to do for you.

Teacher information

Genre:

Letter

Question types and comprehension strategies:

- Analyses and extracts information from a letter to answer literal, deductive and evaluative questions.
- Compares information in a text to own experiences.

Worksheet information:

- A simple letter format is presented on page 35. Commas and full stops are not required at the end of the greeting or the conclusion and the paragraphs are separated by an obvious gap.
- Pupils do not have to base their comparison on page 37 on a bike they actually own. It could be one from their imagination, an older brother's or sister's or one they have seen advertised.

Answers:

Pages 35–36

1. (a) (i) Joel   (ii) Nan and Pop   (iii) a bike
    (b) (i) black, red (ii) grey   (iii) silver
    (c) jumped for joy
    (d) (i)   Joel wrote a letter to his Nan and Pop
        (ii) The bike has a side stand and bell.
        (iii) Joel rode his bike in the park.
2. Teacher check
3. (a) Teacher check   (b) Teacher check

Page 37

Teacher check

Extension:

- Pupils may enjoy having the following series of books read to them:

  The jolly postman (or other people's letters) Janet and Allan Ahlberg

  The jolly pocket postman Janet and Allan Ahlberg

  The jolly Christmas postman Janet and Allan Ahlberg

Thank you – 1

Read the letter.

Dear Nan and Pop

I am writing to thank you both for my wonderful birthday present. When Mum and Dad told me you would like to buy me a bike I jumped for joy! Now I don't have to beg Tyler to let me ride his.

They took me to the bike shop so I could choose. I picked out a red and black one. It has a shiny silver bell and a side stand so I can park it. Mum and Dad bought me a grey bike helmet as another birthday present. I have been riding along the bike path in the park while Mum or Dad take Bonnie for a walk on her lead.

I can't wait to come to the farm in the school holidays. Tyler and I can both ride our bikes along the tracks to the dam and the milking shed. See you soon!

Love Joel

❶ Right there

(a) Answer the questions.

   (i) Who wrote the letter? _______________________

   (ii) Who was the letter written to? _______________________

   (iii) What was the wonderful birthday present? _______________________

(b) Circle the correct word(s).

(i) What colour was the bike?	silver	black	red	grey
(ii) What colour was the helmet?	silver	black	red	grey
(iii) What colour was the bell?	silver	black	red	grey

THANK YOU – 2

Use the text on page 35 to answer the questions.

❶ Right there

(c) Colour the correct words.

When Joel found out he was getting a bike he ...

| screamed and shouted. | jumped for joy. | sang a song. |

(d) Match the beginning of each sentence to its ending.

(i)   Joel wrote a letter to •   • a side stand and bell.

(ii) The bike has •   • in the park.

(iii) Joel rode his bike •   • his Nan and Pop.

❷ Think and search

Answer the questions.

(a) Who do you think Tyler is?

(b) What do you think Bonnie is?

❸ On my own

(a) Draw three things you could see on a farm.

(b) Draw three presents someone your age would like for a birthday.

Primary comprehension   Prim-Ed Publishing   www.prim-ed.com

THANK YOU – 3

Use the text on page 35 to complete the activity.

Complete the empty boxes with words or pictures about your bike or one you would like to own.

	Joel's bike	Your bike
This is a picture of the bike.		
What colour is it?	red and black	
Describe the bell if it has one.	shiny and silver	
Does it have a bike stand?	Yes	
What does the bike helmet look like?	It is grey.	
Where could the bike be ridden?	on the bike track at the park along the tracks at the farm	

Genre:

Science fiction

Question types and comprehension strategies:

- Analyses and extracts information from a science fiction text to answer literal, deductive and evaluative questions.
- Compares information in a text to own experiences.

Worksheet information:

Simple stories can be used to introduce even very young children to a variety of genres. In fact, most will enjoy reading and writing texts in a particular genre. This will stimulate their creativity and imagination.

Answers:

Pages 39–40

1. (a) Teacher check
   (b) Moon Street   robot shop   teleporter
2. (a) John — dad   (b) Sarah — mum
   (c) Alex — oldest boy   (d) Daniel — youngest boy
3. Teacher check

Page 41

Teacher check

Extension:

- Other titles which the pupils may enjoy having read to them include:

  Jed and the space bandits by Jean and Claudio Marzollo

  Commander Toad in space by Jane Yolen

  Aliens for breakfast by Stephanie Spinner and Jonathan Etra

RUSSELL THE ROBOT AND HIS BEST BUDDY – 1

Read the science fiction story.

Russell was a very good robot. He lived with his family—John, Sarah, Alex and Daniel—in a space pod on Moon Street. Alex was the oldest child. He was 13 years old and Daniel was 6. Russell was Daniel's best friend. Alex didn't like to play with Daniel very much, so John bought Russell at the robot shop to look after Daniel. They played 'Fly and seek', 'Robot rescue' and 'Galaxy wars'.

One day when Russell and Daniel were playing, there was a loud 'bang!' and smoke started to come from Russell's metal chest. He came to a sudden stop. Daniel called his mum. She rang the emergency robot service number. In the blink of a star, the serviceman appeared in the teleporter. He fixed Russell and soon Daniel and Russell were playing happily together.

❶ Right there

(a) Draw pictures to match the names.

Russell	Daniel

Russell the Robot and his Best Buddy – 2

Use the text on page 39 to answer the questions.

1 Right there

(b) Find words in the story to label the pictures.

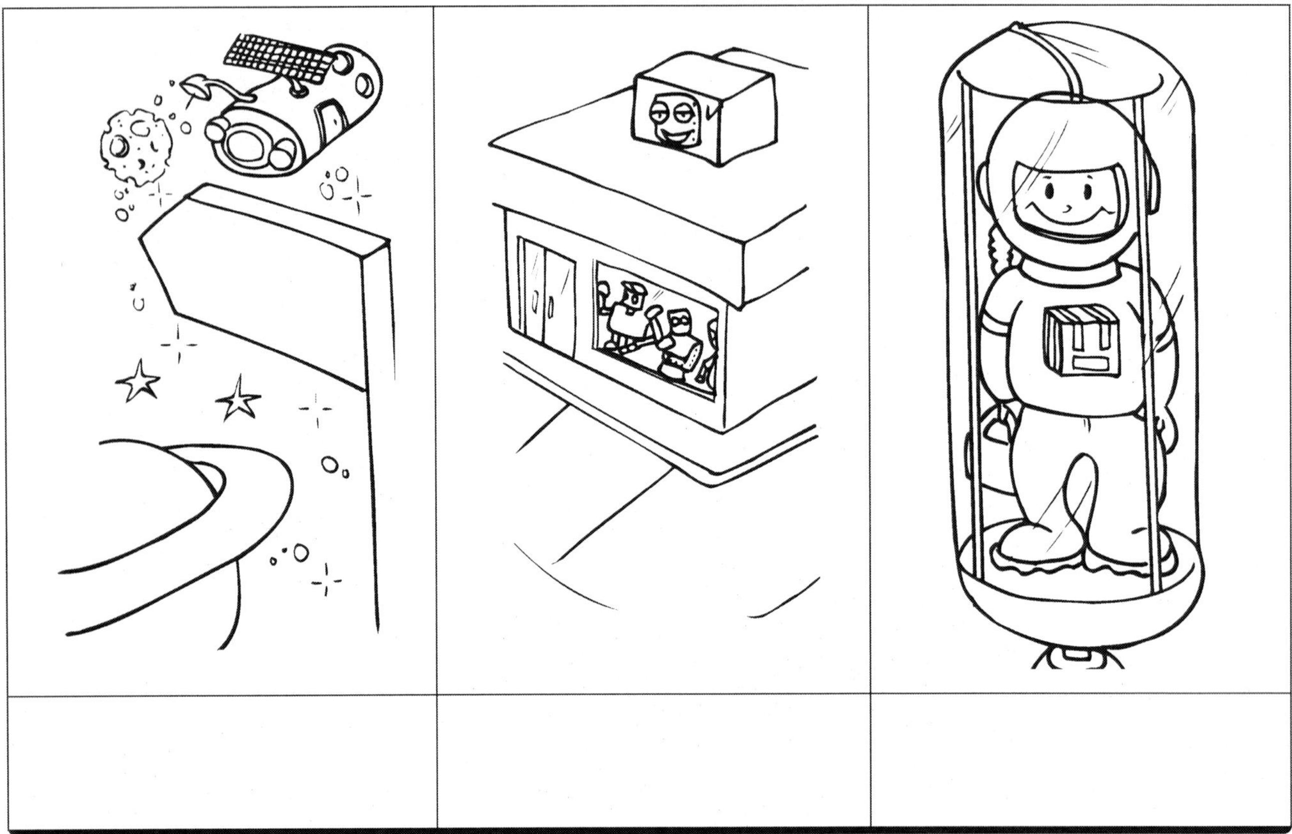

2 Think and search

Match the name to the person.

(a) John   •   • youngest boy

(b) Sarah   •   • oldest boy

(c) Alex   •   • mum

(d) Daniel   •   • dad

3 On my own

Draw or write the names of 5 (five) mechanical things in your house which may need to be fixed.

RUSSELL THE ROBOT AND HIS BEST BUDDY – 3

Use the text on page 39 to make comparisons.

Complete the empty boxes using words or pictures.

Russell's family	Your family
Family members John (dad) Sarah (mum) Alex (big brother) Daniel (younger brother)	Family members
Russell's best friend Daniel (younger brother)	Your best friend
Games played with friends 'Fly and seek' 'Robot rescue' 'Galaxy wars'	Games played with friends
Home space pod on Moon Street	Home
Repairmen who visit robot repairman	Repairmen who visit

Teacher information

Genre:

Poetry

Question types and comprehension strategies:

- Analyses and extracts information from an action rhyme to answer literal, deductive and evaluative questions.
- Uses sensory imaging to create mental images of the actions in a poem.

Worksheet information:

- The activities chosen require very little reading ability; however, adult assistance may be needed at times for the odd unfamiliar word.
- Teachers should read all instructions to the pupils while the pupils point to the words or follow the line of words being read.
- When reading the rhyme with the pupils, it is often helpful to emphasise the rhyming words at the end of the lines and the stressed syllables to help pupils recognise the rhythm.

Answers:

Pages 43–44

1. (a) (i)   The poem tells about things children can do.
   (b) (i) frown   (ii) bite   (iii) bad   (iv) peep
   (c) (i) True   (ii) True
2. (a) Yes   (b) No   (c) Yes   (d) No
3. Teacher check

Page 45

Teacher check

Extension:

- Pupils learn the poem and add their own actions.
- Pupils perform other action rhymes such as *Ten little fingers, Two old tortoises* and action songs such as *Heads, shoulders, knees and toes.*

Action Rhyme – 1

Read the poem.

When I see a laughing clown

My mouth goes up. I do not frown.

When I hug my kitten tight

She turns her head and starts to bite.

When Mum yells and Dad gets mad

The tears run down, 'cause I've been bad.

But when my head goes down to sleep

I close my eyes and do not peep.

❶ Right there

(a) Underline the correct sentence.

   (i) The poem is about things children do.

   (ii) The poem tells a story.

   (iii) The poem is about sad things.

(b) Copy a word from the poem that rhymes with:

   (i) clown ________________

   (ii) tight ________________

   (iii) mad ________________

   (iv) sleep ________________

(c) Colour **True** or **False**.

   (i) The kitten bites when it is hugged too tightly.

     | TRUE | FALSE |

   (ii) The girl in the poem is bad sometimes.

     | TRUE | FALSE |

Action Rhyme – 2

Use the text on page 43 to answer the questions.

❷ Think and search

Colour **Yes** or **No**.

(a) Clowns make the girl happy.   

(b) Kittens like being hugged very tightly.   YES NO

(c) Mum and Dad are trying to help the girl to be well behaved.   YES NO

(d) The girl sleeps poorly at night.   YES NO

❸ On my own

Draw four things which children can do. Write a word to label each picture.

Primary comprehension   Prim-Ed Publishing   www.prim-ed.com

Action Rhyme – 3

Write words or draw pictures to complete
the boxes about the actions in the poem.

(a) When I see a laughing clown, I ...	(b) When I hug a kitten, I ...	(c) When Mum yells and Dad gets mad, I ...	(d) When I am going to sleep, I ...
... can touch ...	... can touch ...	... can touch ...	... can touch ...
... can hear ...	... can hear ...	... can hear ...	... can hear ...
... can smell ...	... can smell ...	... can smell ...	... can smell ...
... see ...	... see ...	... see ...	... see ...

Teacher information

Genre:

Fantasy

Question types and comprehension strategies:

- Analyses and extracts information from a fantasy text to answer literal, deductive and evaluative questions.
- Determines the most important aspects of main characters.

Worksheet information:

- Young children usually love to be read fantasy stories about fairies, goblins, elves, witches and wizards. Fantasy stories encourage children to continue to use their imaginations.
- Ensure that no children are frightened by fantasy characters before reading stories from this genre. Stories should be simple — not horrific or scary.

Answers:

Pages 47–48

1. (a) (i) William   (ii) Wanda   (iii) (It was her) birthday
   (iv) gift box
   (b) (i) sun   (ii) sparkles   (iii) trees
   (iv) wonderful
2. (a) Yes   (b) Yes   (c) No   (d) Yes
3. Teacher check

Page 49

Teacher check

Extension:

- Other titles which the pupils may enjoy having read to them include:

  Winnie the witch by Korky Paul and Valerie Thomas

  Room on the broom by Julia Donaldson

  The spiffiest giant in town by Julia Donaldson

  Big pumpkin by Erica Silverman

THE WONDERFUL BIRTHDAY GIFT – 1

Read the fantasy story.

William sat on his wizard bed and began to think.

In two days, it was going to be his friend, Wanda's, birthday. Wanda was a very lucky witch. Her parents loved her very much and she had all the toys she wanted. William wanted to give her a special gift that no-one else would give her. He thought and thought. At last he had an idea!

The day of Wanda's party arrived. William had a big grin on his face when he gave Wanda her gift box.

'You'll have to wait until the sun goes down to open your present!', he said.

When all the guests had gone home, William watched from his bedroom window as the sun went down. He could see Wanda in her bedroom looking at the box.

Suddenly, the box burst open. Sparkles of rainbow-coloured dust flew into the air, circled Wanda's head and fell onto the trees outside Wanda's window. They glowed and twinkled in the darkness.

'What a wonderful gift!' she said. 'The best one I've ever had! Now I have my own stars to light up the night right outside my bedroom window!'

William just smiled to himself.

❶ Right there

(a) Copy a word from the story to answer the questions.

   (i)   What was the wizard's name? ______________________

   (ii) What was the name of his best friend? ______________________

   (iii) Why was Wanda having a party? ______________________

   (iv) What did William give Wanda? ______________________

THE WONDERFUL BIRTHDAY GIFT – **2**

Use the text on page 47 to answer the questions.

1 Right there

(b) Write a word from the list to complete the sentences.

sparkles	wonderful	sun	trees

(i) Wanda had to wait until the _________________ went down to open her present.

(ii) The box was filled with _________________.

(iii) The sparkles landed on the _________________ outside Wanda's window.

(iv) Wanda thought the gift was _________________.

2 Think and search

Colour **Yes** or **No** to answer the questions.

(a) William liked Wanda.
YES
NO

(b) William wanted to give Wanda a nice present because she was his friend.
YES
NO

(c) Wanda was told not to open her gift until the sun went down because it was not as good as the other gifts.
YES
NO

(d) William was happy that Wanda liked her gift.
YES
NO

3 On my own

Draw and label the best gift you have been given.

THE WONDERFUL BIRTHDAY GIFT – 3

Use the text on page 47 to complete the questions.

Draw a picture and write words to tell about William and Wanda.

William, the wizard

I am ...

I like ...

People like me mostly because ...

Wanda, the witch

I am ...

I like ...

People like me mostly because ...

Teacher information

Genre:

Myth

Question types and comprehension strategies:

- Analyses and extracts information from a myth to answer literal, deductive and evaluative questions.
- Determines the importance of events in a myth to summarise and retell the story.

Worksheet information:

Before pupils complete the summarising activity on page 53, either independently or in pairs, read through the story several times with the pupils and have them suggest the beginning, the events in the middle and finally the ending. They will need to make a decision on how to summarise the events in the middle into just two.

Answers:

Pages 51–52

1. (a) (i) golden   (ii) seaweed   (iii) cave
   (b) picture of the sun
   (c) picture of a rock
   (d) (i) The mermaid sang about a golden light.
       (ii) Clytie swam to the surface to see the golden light.
       (iii) The golden light was the sun.
   (e) (i) petals   (ii) roots   (iii) leaves
2. (a) Yes   (b) No   (c) No
3. Teacher check

Page 53

Teacher check

Extension:

- Books containing myths suitable for this age group are:
  Greek myths for young children by Heather Amery
  15 Greek myth mini-books by Danielle Blood
  Classic myths to read aloud by William F Russell

THE SUNFLOWER – 1

Read the myth.

Once upon a time there was a beautiful nymph called Clytie. She lived in a cave at the bottom of the sea. Clytie had long golden hair. She wore a green gown made of seaweed.

One day, Clytie heard a mermaid singing. Her song was about a golden light that shone above the water. Clytie longed to see this wonderful light.

She decided to swim to the surface and climb onto a rock. There she saw the wonderful golden light. It was the sun! She sat looking at it all that day, the next day and the next.

At last she looked down and into the water. Then she saw that her hair had become yellow petals. Her green gown had become leaves. Her tiny feet had become roots. Clytie had become a sunflower!

If you look closely at a sunflower, you will see that it turns its face to follow the sun as it moves across the sky.

❶ Right there

(a) Circle the correct word.

    (i) What colour was Clytie's hair?

| green | golden | yellow |

    (ii) What was her gown made of?

| reeds | petals | seaweed |

    (iii) What did she live in?

| cave | rock | house |

(b) Draw what Clytie wanted to see.

(c) Draw what Clytie sat on.

THE SUNFLOWER – 2

Use the text on page 51 to answer the questions.

❶ Right there

(d) Match the beginning of the sentence to its ending.

(i) The mermaid sang about •   • was the sun.

(ii) Clytie swam to the surface •   • a golden light.

(iii) The golden light •   • to see the golden light.

(e) Clytie became a sunflower. Write what each part of her turned into.

(i) Her hair turned into

_______________________.

(ii) Her feet turned into

_______________________.

(iii) Her gown turned into

_______________________.

❷ Think and search

Colour **yes** or **no**.

(a) Clytie looked at the sun for three days. YES NO

(b) A sunflower is an animal. YES NO

(c) Clytie had been to the surface lots of times. YES NO

❸ On my own

What is wrong with this picture? Draw how it should look in the blank box.

THE SUNFLOWER – 3

Use the text on page 51 to complete the activity.

Draw a picture and write words in each box to show what happened in each part of the story.

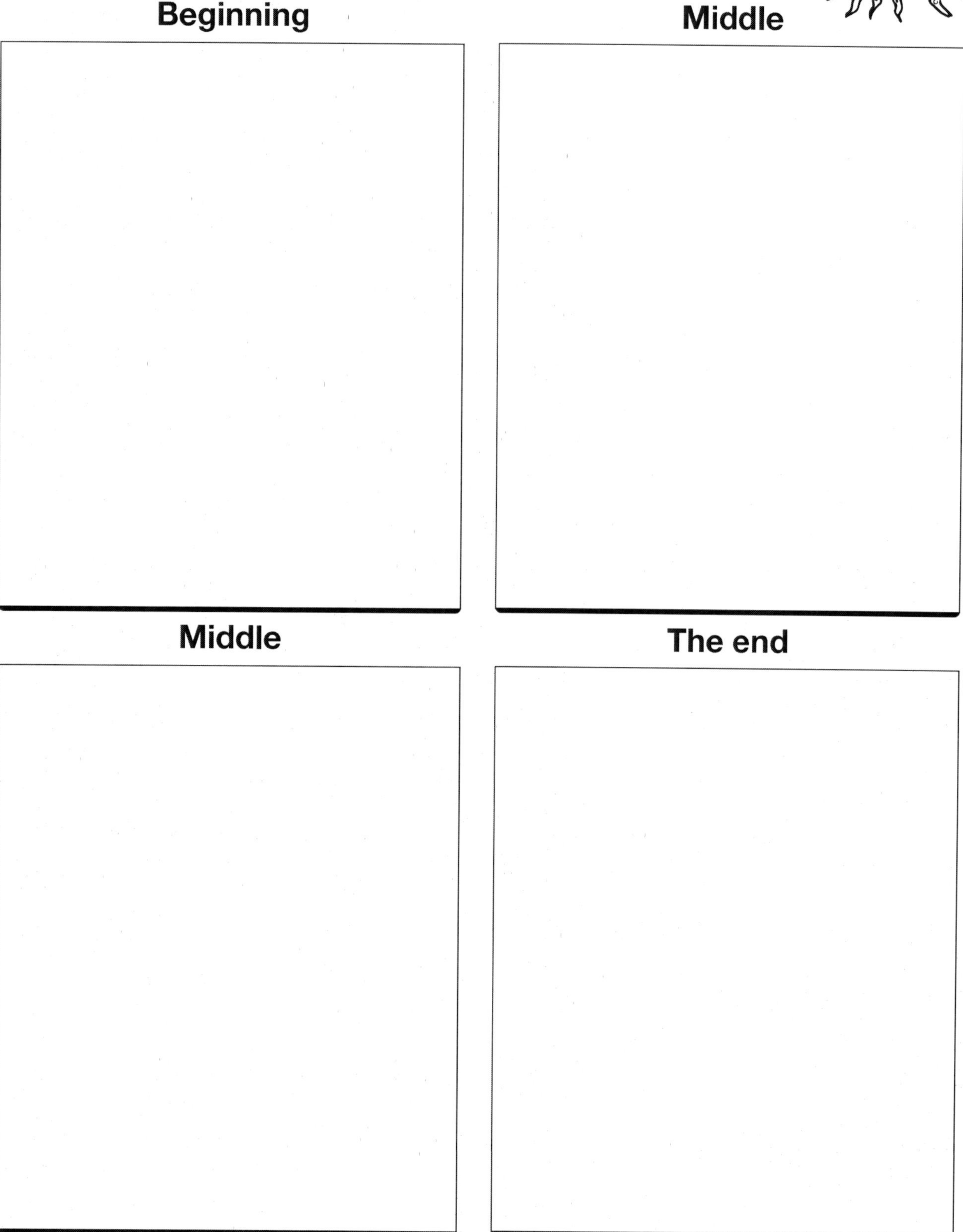

Beginning

Middle

Middle

The end

Retell the story to a friend.

THE RAVEN AND THE SWAN

Teacher information

Genre:

Fable

Question types and comprehension strategies:

- Analyses and extracts information from a fable to answer literal, deductive and evaluative questions.
- Scans a text to locate words.

Worksheet information:

- The fable chosen was written by Aesop and may be unfamiliar to the children. Explain that a fable is a story with a moral. (It tries to teach the reader something!)
- Encourage pupils to follow and try to read the words as they are being read to them.

Answers:

Pages 55–56

1. (a) (i) False (ii) False (iii) True (iv) True (v) True
   (b) (i) lake (ii) beautiful (iii) day (iv) black (v) eat

2. (a) The raven had black feathers.
   (b) He thought that he was ugly and the swan was beautiful.
   (c) He wanted to be close to the lake where the swan lived.
   (d) He thought the water would turn them white and he would be beautiful like the swan.

3. Teacher check

Page 57

1. (a) white (b) black (c) feathers (d) beautiful
   (e) home (f) day (g) eat

2. Teacher check

Extension:

- Other fables by Aesop which may be read to pupils include:
  The ant and the grasshopper
  The hare and the tortoise
  The lion and the mouse
  The fox and the grapes
- Pupils may discuss the moral of the fable.

THE RAVEN AND THE SWAN – 1

Read the fable.

A black raven saw a beautiful white swan washing her feathers in the water while she was swimming. The raven wanted to be as beautiful as the swan.

The raven left his home and went to live near the lake where the swan lived. He cleaned his feathers every day in the water but his feathers did not change from black to white. He spent so much time trying to make himself beautiful that he did not eat and soon died.

❶ Right there

(a) Colour **True** or **False**.

   (i) The raven was white.

      | TRUE | FALSE |

   (ii) The swan was black.

      | TRUE | FALSE |

   (iii) The swan was beautiful.

      | TRUE | FALSE |

   (iv) The raven thought he was ugly.

      | TRUE | FALSE |

   (v) The raven died.

      | TRUE | FALSE |

(b) Colour the correct word.

   (i) The swan lived near the

      | sea | lake | .

   (ii) The swan was

      | ugly | beautiful | .

   (iii) The raven washed his feathers every

      | night | day | .

   (iv) The raven's feathers stayed | white | black | .

   (v) The raven did not

      | wash | eat | .

THE RAVEN AND THE SWAN – **2**

Use the text on page 55 to answer the questions.

Write sentences to answer the questions.

(a) What colour feathers did the raven have?

____

(b) Why did the raven want to be like the swan?

____

(c) Why did the raven leave his own home?

____

(d) What did the raven think the water would do to his feathers?

____

Draw two birds which look very different but are both still beautiful.
Label each with its name if you can.

THE RAVEN AND THE SWAN – **3**

Use the text on page 55 to answer the questions.

❶ Copy a word from the fable to finish the sentences.

(a) The swan had _________________________ feathers.

(b) The raven had _________________________ feathers.

(c) The swan was washing her _______________ in the water.

(d) The raven wanted to be as _______________ as the swan.

(e) The raven left his _______________.

(f) The raven washed his feathers every _______________.

(g) The raven did not _______________ so he died.

❷ Write three different words from the fable which begin with the letter in the box.

s	**w**	**b**

Teacher information

Genre:

Folktale

Question types and comprehension strategies:

- Analyses and extracts information from a folktale to answer literal, deductive and evaluative questions.
- Scans text to identify relevant events.
- Uses synthesis to recall information and order details to sequence a story.

Worksheet information:

This story is based on a Norwegian folktale, though there are similar tales about bears in other countries. The folktale warns of believing something too readily without looking into the 'big picture'.

Answers:

Pages 59–60

1. (a) (iii) The story is about how the bear got a stumpy tail.
   (b) long, bushy
   (c) (i) fox, fish   (ii) pull, jerk   (iii) tail, frozen
2. (a) yes   (b) yes   (c) no   (d) no
3. Teacher check

Page 61

Teacher check

Extension:

- Pupils may enjoy listening to other folktales concerning how or why something is so. Some titles are:

  How the kangaroo got its pouch

  How the echidna got its spines

  Why the bat has no friends

  How the sky came to be

- Rudyard Kipling has a collection of *Just so* stories. Titles include:

  How the whale got its throat

  How the leopard got its spots

  How the rhinoceros got its skin

WHY THE BEAR HAS A STUMPY TAIL – 1

Read the folktale.

Long ago, the bear had a long, bushy tail like a fox. One day, the bear met a fox. The fox had some fish he had stolen.

'Where did you get the fish?' asked the bear.

'I caught them', said the fox.

'How did you catch them?' asked the bear.

'Oh, it's easy. Just cut a hole in the ice and stick your long tail into it. Hold it there as long as you can. The fish will bite your tail and hold on. Then you pull up your tail with a strong jerk.'

So the bear did what the fox said. He held his tail down a long, long time in the cold, cold water. His tail became frozen. At last he pulled his tail up. It snapped off!

And that is why the bear has a stumpy tail.

❶ Right there

(a)   Underline the correct sentence.

   (i)   The story is about how the fox got a stumpy tail.

   (ii)   The story is about how to fish.

   (iii)   The story is about how the bear got a stumpy tail.

(b)   Colour the words that say what the bear's tail looked like long ago.

long	stumpy	short	bushy	little

WHY THE BEAR HAS A STUMPY TAIL – 2

Use the text on page 59 to answer the questions.

❶ Right there

(c) Complete the sentences by copying words from the story.

(i) The bear asked the _______________ where he got the

_______________.

(ii) The fox told the bear to _______________ up his tail with a

strong _______________.

(iii) The bear held his _______________ in the water for so

long it became _______________.

❷ Think and search

Colour **yes** or **no**.

(a) The fox told lies.   

(b) The bear believed the fox.   

(c) The bear caught some fish.   

(d) The fox helped the bear pull his tail up.

❸ On my own

Draw another way the bear could have caught some fish.

WHY THE BEAR HAS A STUMPY TAIL – **3**

Use the text on page 59 to complete the activity.

(a) Draw the missing pictures from the story.

(b) Colour and cut out the pictures and put them in the correct order to tell the story.

Teacher information

Genre:

Humour (poem)

Question types and comprehension strategies:

- Analyses and extracts information from a humorous poem to answer literal, deductive and evaluative questions.
- Synthesises and completes details about the events in a humorous poem to show order.

Worksheet information:

- There are unfamiliar words in this poem which will be too hard for many children to read. It is suggested that the teacher read the poem to the pupils while they follow with their fingers.
- Humour may be written in story or poetry form.
- Pupils can write about a friend's pet or an imaginary pet to answer Question 3 on page 64 if they have no pet of their own.

Answers:

Pages 63–64

1. (a) Mr Grumble, Tilly Tidy-up, cat, dog, mouse
   (b) (i)   Tilly made cakes, buns and drinks.
       (ii) Tilly put the cat and dog safely out of sight.
       (iii) The cat and dog chased the mouse.
       (iv) The food and dishes fell in a heap.
2. (a) False   (b) True   (c) False
3. Teacher check

Page 65

1. 2, 1, 3, 4, 6, 5, 7
2. Teacher check

Extension:

- Other titles which the pupils may enjoy having read to them include:

  Olivia by Ian Falconer

  Giraffes can't dance by Giles Andrede and Guy Parker Rees

  The Berenstein Bears stories by Stan and Jan Berenstein

- Read 'Knock, knock' jokes to the pupils and allow them to tell or write some of their own.

TILLY TIDY-UP – 1

Read the humorous poem.

Tilly Tidy-up was in a tizzy.

The house was so clean that Tilly was dizzy.

The food was ready. The drinks were poured.

Soon the guests would knock at the door.

The cat and dog — her heart's delight

Were safely placed out of sight.

None of her guests would hear a peep

As they ate their cake and rested their feet.

The time was passing happily.

The guests were chatting noisily.

When soon was heard a squeaking sound

And chaos then was all around.

The mouse sped in – the cat behind.

The dog came next in record time.

Round and round the tabletop

The animals ran — and did not stop.

Food and dishes fell in a heap.

All the guests began to shriek.

Mr Grumble, loud and round

Began to laugh and Tilly soon found

That all were having so much fun

They even ate the mushy buns.

TILLY TIDY-UP – 2

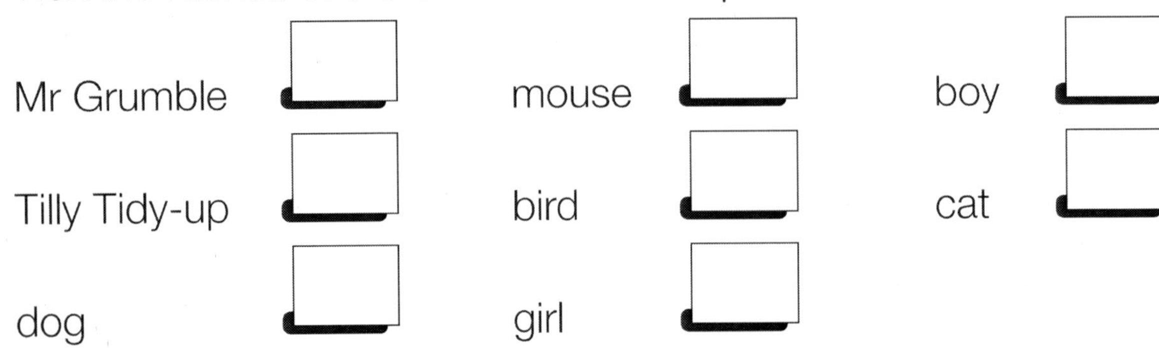

Use the text on page 63 to answer the questions.

❶ Right there

(a) Tick the names of the characters in the poem.

Mr Grumble ☐   mouse ☐   boy ☐

Tilly Tidy-up ☐   bird ☐   cat ☐

dog ☐   girl ☐

(b) Join the beginning of the sentence to its ending.

(i)   Tilly made   •   • safely out of sight.

(ii) Tilly put the cat and dog   •   • cake, buns and drinks.

(iii) The cat and dog chased   •   • in a heap.

(iv) The food and dishes fell   •   • the mouse.

❷ Think and search

Colour **True** or **False** to answer the questions.

(a) Tilly did not love her cat and dog.

TRUE | FALSE

(b) The pets were put away so that they would not disturb the guests.

TRUE | FALSE

(c) Mr Grumble was thin.

TRUE | FALSE

❸ On my own

Draw a picture or write words to tell about a time when your pet got into mischief.

Tilly Tidy-up – 3

Use the text on page 63 to complete the questions.

1 Write the numbers 1 to 7 next to each event to show the order in which they happened.

Tilly puts out the food and drink.

Tilly cleans up.

Tilly puts the cat and dog away.

The guests eat their food.

The food and drink fall into a heap.

The cat and dog chase the mouse around the table.

The guests laugh and eat mushy buns.

2 Draw pictures to match the sentences.

Teacher information

Genre:

Procedure

Question types and comprehension strategies:

- Analyses and extracts information from a procedure to answer literal, deductive and evaluative questions.
- Scans text to identify relevant events.
- Uses synthesis to recall information and order details to sequence a procedure.

Worksheet information:

Although the pizza does not need to be made to complete the activities, teachers or pupils could demonstrate each step in making the pizza as a stimulus or to assist in understanding.

Answers:

Pages 67–68

1. (a) (i) Lebanese   (ii) pizza sauce   (iii) grated cheese
   (b) four
   (c) (i)   The pizza is put on an oven tray.
       (ii) The ham and pineapple are chopped into pieces.
       (iii) The cheese is grated.
2. Teacher check
3. Teacher check

Page 69

Teacher check

Extension:

- Pupils draw and write simple steps to explain how to make a milkshake, a sandwich, a fruit salad or a recipe of their own choice for others to sequence.
- Pupils make the pizza as directed or the one they drew the ingredients for in Question 3 on page 68. After tasting, they could rate it from 1 to 5 and suggest improvements if necessary.

HOW TO MAKE A PIZZA – 1

Read the procedure.

You will need:

- *oven tray*
- *pizza sauce*
- *Lebanese bread*
- *grated cheese*
- *pineapple pieces*
- *sliced tomato*
- *sliced onion*
- *sliced pepper*
- *sliced mushroom*
- *chopped ham*

Method:

1. *Spread pizza sauce over the Lebanese bread.*

2. *Top with sliced tomato, onion, pepper and mushroom.*

3. *Add chopped ham and pineapple pieces.*

4. *Sprinkle with grated cheese.*

5. *Put on an oven tray.*

6. *Cook in a hot oven until the cheese is melted and browned.*

❶ Right there

Answer the questions.

(a) Choose words from the procedure.

   (i) What kind of bread was used? _______________________

   (ii) What was spread on the bread? _______________________

   (iii) What was sprinkled on the pizza? _______________________

(b) Colour the number of things that were sliced.

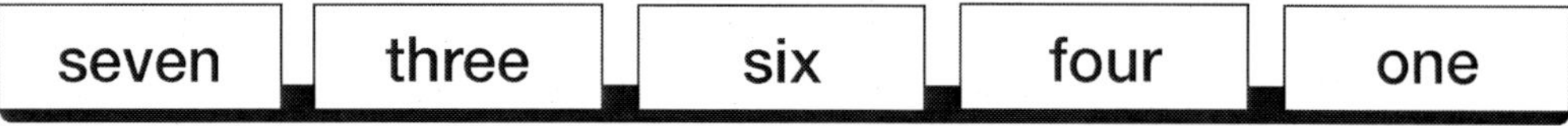

seven	three	six	four	one

HOW TO MAKE A PIZZA – **2**

Use the text on page 67 to answer the questions.

❶ Right there

(c) Match each sentence beginning to its ending.

    (i)   The pizza is put   •   • is grated.

    (ii) The ham and pineapple •   • on an oven tray.

    (iii) The cheese   •   • are chopped into pieces.

❷ Think and search

List four fruits or vegetables that were put on the pizza.

______________________________   ______________________________

______________________________   ______________________________

❸ On my own

(a) Tick the things you would like on a pizza. Add any others.

(b) Draw what you would like to put on a pizza.

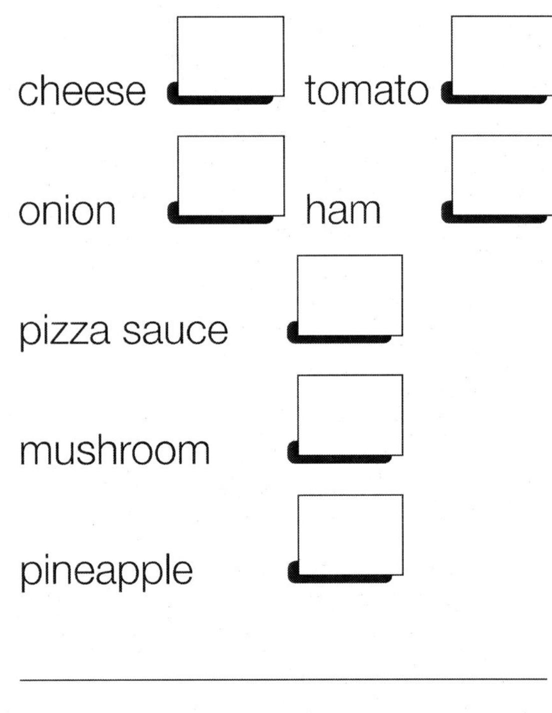

cheese ☐   tomato ☐

onion ☐   ham ☐

pizza sauce ☐

mushroom ☐

pineapple ☐

____

____

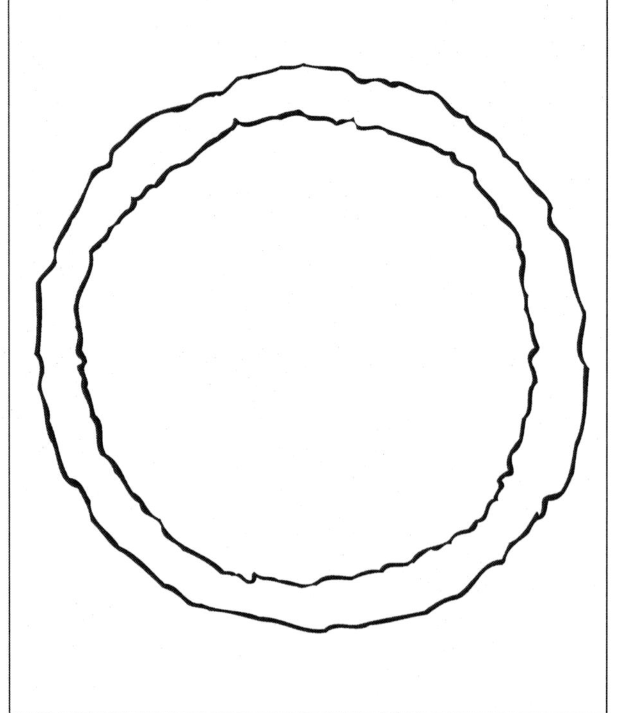

Primary comprehension   Prim-Ed Publishing   www.prim-ed.com

HOW TO MAKE A PIZZA – **3**

Use the text on page 67 to complete the activity.

(a) Draw the missing pictures and write the missing sentences about how to make a pizza.

(b) Colour and cut them out and put them in the correct order.

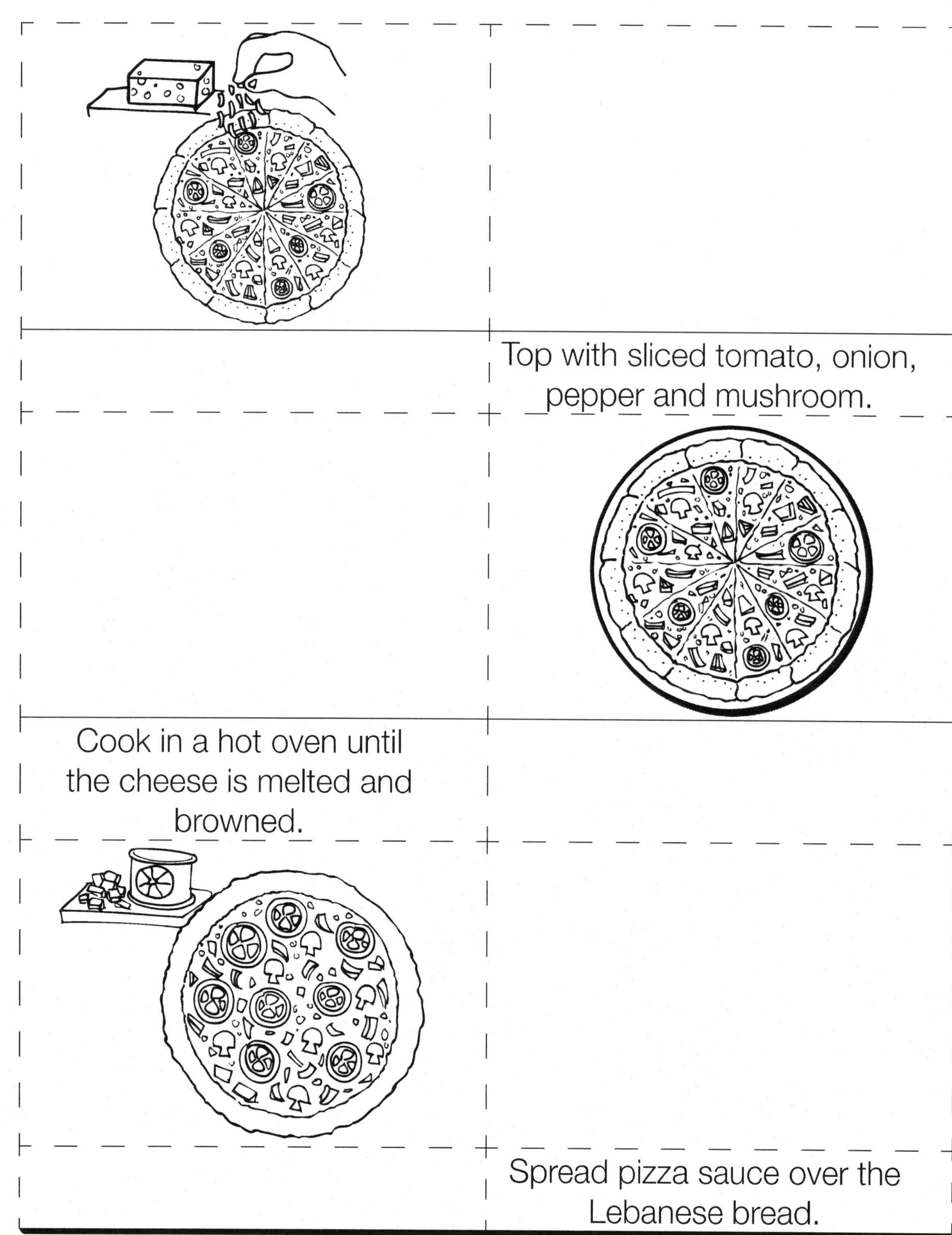

Teacher information

Genre:

Cartoon – visual text

Question types and comprehension strategies:

- Analyses and extracts information from a cartoon to answer literal, deductive and evaluative questions.
- Summarises information in a cartoon by drawing a life cycle diagram.

Worksheet information:

- Pupils should know the difference between a deciduous and an evergreen tree before completing pages 72 and 73.
- Pupils will need some understanding of simple life cycles such as those of a frog or butterfly to enable Question 3 on page 72 to be answered.

Answers:

Page 72

1. (a) Bill, Ben (b) autumn (c) winter (d) spring (e) odd
2. (a) deciduous (b) evergreen (c) cold (d) summer (e) happy
3. Teacher check

Page 73

Teacher check

Extension:

- Other titles about life cycles which the pupils may enjoy reading include:

  The very hungry caterpillar by Eric Carle

  Alfie's long winter by Greg McEvoy

  Squiggly Wiggly's surprise by Arnold Shapiro

  A butterfly is born by Melvin Berger
- Read nonfiction books about seasons and changes in animals and plants.

CARTOON – 1

Read the cartoon.

CARTOON – 2

❶ Right there

Copy words from the cartoon on page 71 to answer the questions.

(a) What are the names of the two trees?

_________________________ and _________________________

(b) When did Ben start to lose his leaves?_________________________

(c) When did Ben have bare branches? _________________________

(d) When did Ben start to grow new leaves?_________________________

(e) How did Bill think Ben looked without leaves? _________________________

❷ Think and search

Circle the correct words.

(a) Ben is a/an | *evergreen* | *deciduous* | tree.

(b) Bill is a/an | *deciduous* | *evergreen* |

tree.

(c) In winter, the weather is | *cold* | *hot* |.

(d) Ben has all his leaves back by | *spring* | *summer* |.

(e) Bill was | *happy* | *sad* |
that he had leaves all year
round.

❸ On my own

Draw pictures or write words to show how an egg can change into an animal.

Cartoon – 3

Use the cartoon on page 71 to complete a drawing of the life cycle of a deciduous tree.

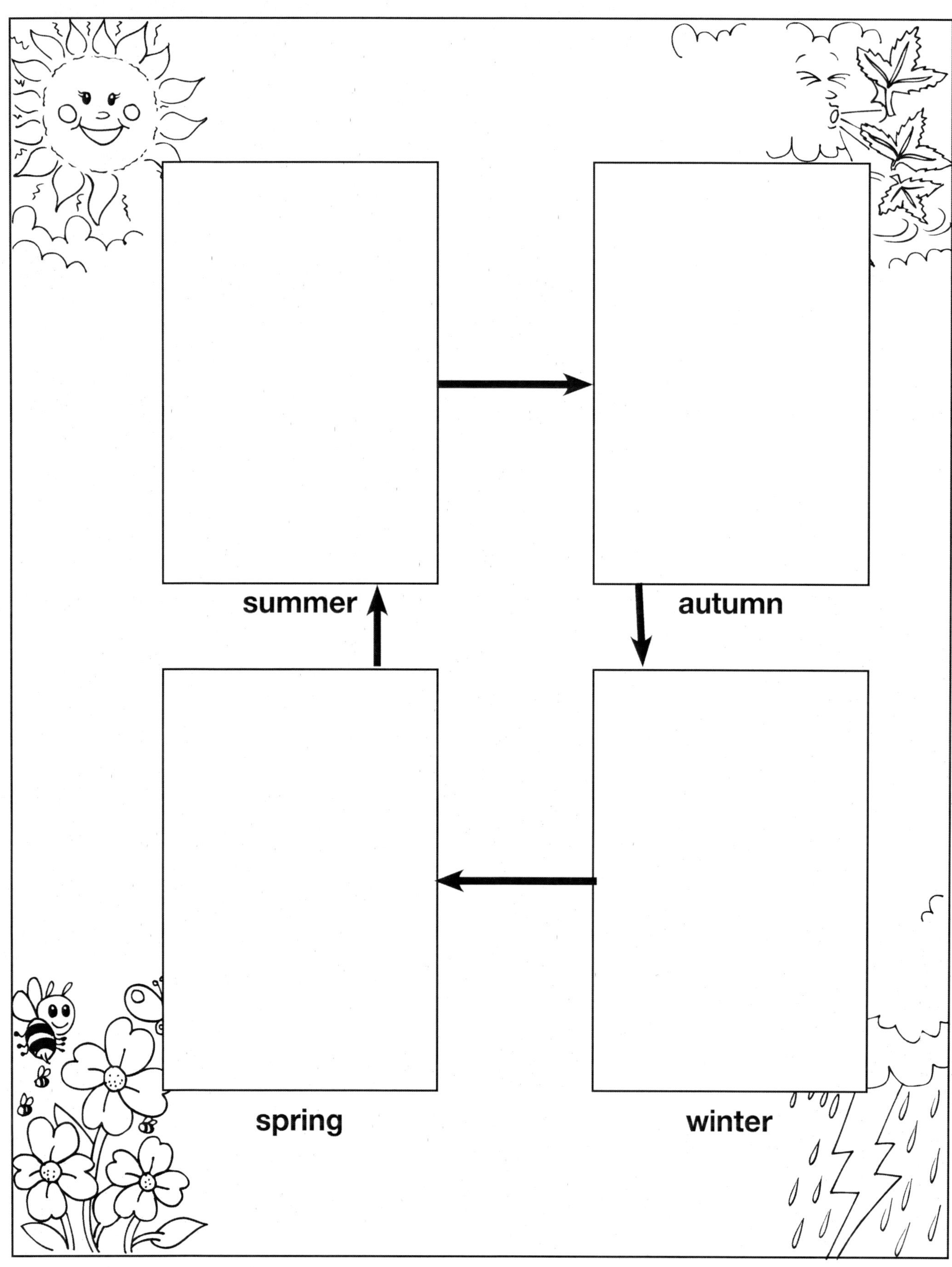

Teacher information

Genre:

Report

Question types and comprehension strategies:

- Analyses and extracts information from a report to answer literal, deductive and evaluative questions.
- Scans text to determine important information.
- Summarises text by recording keywords and phrases.

Worksheet information:

Pupils could use different colours to highlight keywords needed to complete the chart on page 77. The activity is suitable for working in pairs.

Answers:

Pages 75–76

1. (a) elephant, largest, lives
   (b) (i) 4   (ii) 2   (iii) 2   (iv) 1
   (c) (i) No   (ii) No   (iii) Yes   (iv) Yes
2. fruit
3. (a) (i) lamb   (ii) puppy   (iii) calf   (iv) kitten
   (b) Teacher check

Page 77

Teacher check

Extension:

- Pupils may enjoy having books about animal facts read to them from the following series:

  Animal books for young children published by Acorn Naturalists

  The faces of nature series by Mymi Doinet

  Wild, wild world series by Tanya Lee Stone

THE ELEPHANT – 1

Read the report.

The elephant is the largest animal that lives on land. It has four strong legs and feet that are almost round. Its skin is grey and wrinkled. The elephant has two very large ears. It has a long trunk and two pointy white tusks. Its tail is thin.

The elephant likes to live in a group. It eats grass, leaves, bark and fruit. The elephant uses its trunk to put food and water into its mouth. It also uses it to spray water over its back.

A baby elephant is called a calf. An elephant can live for about 65 years.

❶ Right there

(a) Fill in the missing words. | largest | lives | elephant |

The ______________ is the ______________ animal that

______________ on land.

(b) Write the correct number.

(i) How many legs does an elephant have?

(ii) How many tusks does an elephant have?

(iii) How many ears does an elephant have?

(iv) How many tails does an elephant have?

THE ELEPHANT – 2

Use the text on page 75 to answer the questions.

❶ Right there

(c) Colour **yes** or **no**.

(i)   An elephant has smooth skin.   YES | NO

(ii)   A baby elephant is a cub.   YES | NO

(iii) An elephant likes to live in a group.   YES | NO

(iv) An elephant can live for about 65 years.   YES | NO

❷ Think and search

What food could you eat that an elephant likes to eat?

____

❸ On my own

(a) Can you guess the correct word? | *puppy* | *calf* | *kitten* | *lamb* |

(i)   A baby sheep is called a _____________________.

(ii)   A baby dog is called a _____________________.

(iii) A baby cow is called a _____________________.

(iv) A baby cat is called a _____________________.

(b) Draw two animals that are almost as large as the elephant.

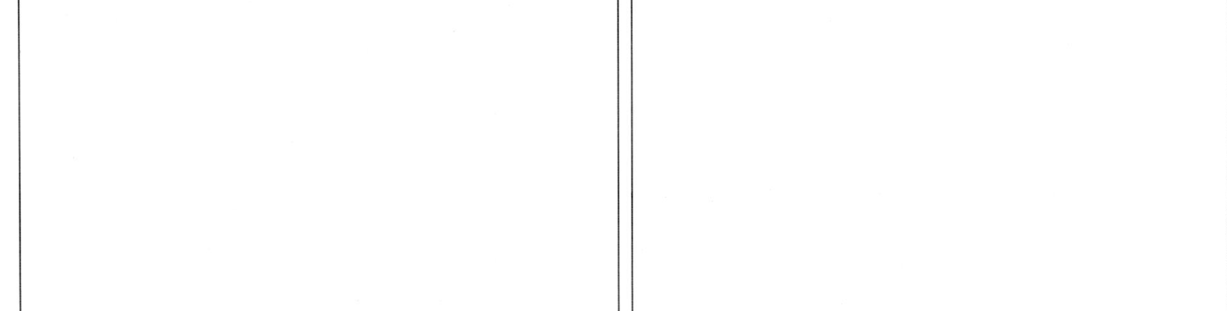

Primary comprehension   Prim-Ed Publishing   www.prim-ed.com

THE ELEPHANT – 3

Use the text on page 75 to complete the activity.

Find words in the report about the elephant to complete the chart.

The elephant

What does it look like?

| ears ... | legs and feet ... |

| trunk ... | skin ... |

| tusks ... | tail ... |

What does it eat?

| Draw something it likes to do. | An interesting fact |

Teacher information

Genre:

Adventure

Question types and comprehension strategies:

- Analyses and extracts information from an adventure story to answer literal, deductive and evaluative questions.
- Scans text to identify relevant events.
- Completes a story map to summarise main events.

Worksheet information:

The story map activity on page 81 is a useful way of summarising important events in a story. It is too difficult at this level for pupils to plan and draw an entire map, so adding missing details by referring to the text is a helpful method. Pupils can outline the movement of the main characters after the map is complete and retell the story from their map.

Answers:

Pages 79–80

1.   (a)   (i)   My grandad lives next to the wild woods.

           (ii)   We like to walk in the woods.

           (iii)   I hold on to his hand.

    (b)   (i)   2   (ii)   10   (iii)   10

    (c)   (i)   Yes   (ii)   No   (iii)   No   (iv)   No

2–3.   Teacher check

Page 81

Teacher check

Extension:

- Pupils could retell the story, adding a different character, deleting a character or changing the ending.
- Fairytales such as *The three little pigs*, *Goldilocks and the three bears*, *The gingerbread man* and *Little Red Riding Hood* are suitable for story map activities. Another popular title ideal for a story map is *Rosie's walk* by Pat Hutchins.

A WALK IN THE WOODS – 1

Read the adventure.

My grandad lives next to the wild woods. I hold on to his hand when we walk in the woods. What will happen this time?

We walk along the winding path. We see a nest in a tree. We tiptoe past two baby birds. We climb over a little log. We count ten tiny toadstools on the grass. We look at a busy bee. We say hello to a wriggling worm. We run past a speedy spider. We step over a big puddle. We find ten tadpoles in a pond. Then ...

CROAK! QUACK! WHAT IS THAT?

We hold hands tightly.

Oh! It's just a friendly frog and a diving duck.

We say goodbye. We walk back along the winding path.

❶ Right there

(a) Match each sentence beginning to its ending.

    (i)   My grandad lives •   • to his hand.

    (ii) We like to •   • next to the wild woods.

    (iii) I hold on •   • walk in the woods.

(b) Write the correct number.

    (i)   How many birds did they see?

    (ii) How many tadpoles did they see?

    (iii) How many toadstools did they see?

A WALK IN THE WOODS – 2

Use the text on page 79 to answer the questions.

❶ Right there

(c) Colour **yes** or **no**.

(i) They see a nest in a tree.
   YES / NO

(ii) They trip over a log.
   YES / NO

(iii) They say hello to a speedy spider.
   YES / NO

(iv) They fall in a puddle.
   YES / NO

❷ Think and search

(a) Colour the animal that said CROAK green and the animal that said QUACK yellow.

| spider | duck | bee | worm | frog |

(b) When Grandad and the child hear a CROAK and a QUACK they hold hands tightly. Why?

____

____

____

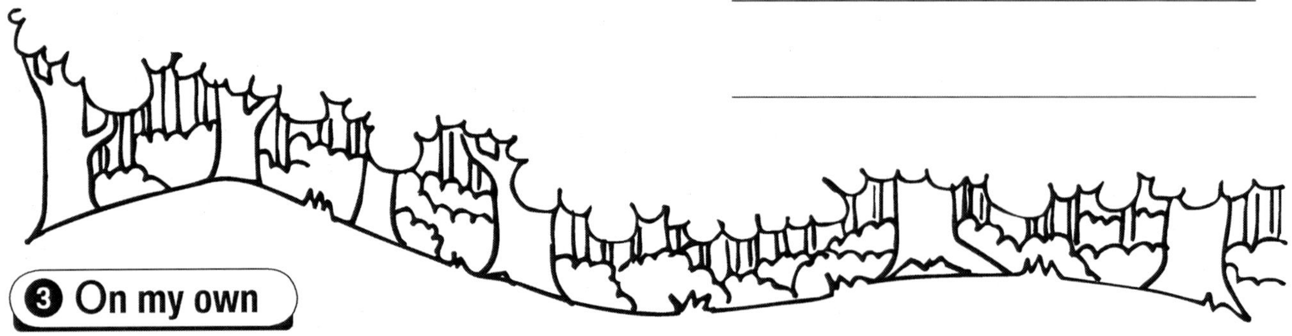

❸ On my own

(a) Draw what you would like to happen most if you went for a walk in the woods.

(b) Draw what you would not like to happen if you went for a walk in the woods.

A <u>WALK IN THE WOODS – 3</u>

Use the text on page 79 to complete the activity.

(a)   Draw the missing pictures to finish the story map.

(b)   Then draw a path to show the walk in the woods.

(c)   Tell the story to a friend.